THE MILL GIRLS

THE MILL GIRLS

A view of Lowell, Massachusetts,

Lucy Larcom
Harriet Hanson Robinson
Sarah G. Bagley

by BERNICE SELDEN

ATHENEUM 1983 NEW YORK

showing the mills along the river.

PICTURE CREDITS

Beverly Historical Society 15, 25
Boston Public Library 75, 111, 166
Essex Institute 19, 46, 59
Lowell Historical Society 4, 22, 31, 70–71
Lowell Museum 1
Merrimack Valley Textile Museum, title page, 8, 36, 77, 84,
89, 122–123, 124, 127, 145, 149, 170–171
Schlesinger Library, Radcliffe College 80, 93, 96
University of Lowell 10, 163

LIBRARY OF CONGRESS CATALOGING IN PUBLICATION DATA

Selden, Bernice.   The mill girls.

Bibliography
Includes index
1. Women textile workers—Massachusetts—
Lowell—Biography.   2. Lowell (Mass.)—Biography.
3. Larcom, Lucy, 1824-1893.
4. Robinson, Harriet H. (Harriet Hanson), 1825-1911.
5. Bagley, Sarah G.
I. Title.
HD6073.T42U57   1983   331.4'877'00922 [B]   83-2672
ISBN 0-689-31005-6

Copyright © 1983 by Bernice Selden
All rights reserved
Published simultaneously in Canada by
McClelland & Stewart, Ltd.
Text set by
Maryland Linotype Composition, Baltimore, Maryland
Printed and bound by
Fairfield Graphics, Fairfield, Pennsylvania
Designed by Mary Ahern
First Edition

For
HERMAN PASSKOW

and in memory of
DOROTHY OSOFSKY
(1926–1983)

Author's Note

SOME OF MY NOTES are yellow with age and the old photostats are fading and getting blurry. I began my research on Lucy Larcom in the early 1960s, intrigued by this cameo life, so modest and yet so purposeful. In my mind I called the book A Woman of the Century, because Lucy had done the most a woman could do, given the restrictions of time and circumstance.

Eventually my project expanded to include two other lives that would flesh out the picture of a remarkable period in American history. Harriet Robinson emerged from her lifelong struggle for survival to become an activist in the woman suffrage movement. And Sarah Bagley—that woman of mystery!—organized the unorganized, all working women, at a time when labor was just beginning to feel its strength.

The work of Helena Wright and Claudia L. Bushman provided invaluable spadework on the Bagley and Robinson fronts. The staffs of the Beverly Historical Society, the Beverly Public Library, Essex

Institute, Lowell University's Special Collections, the Massachusetts Historical Society, the Merrimack Valley Textile Museum and the Wheaton College Library were inordinately helpful over the years.

I am grateful to the YIVO Institute for Jewish Research (where I work part time as a slide curator) for its efforts in procuring research materials from distant places.

And my family and friends—what would I have done without them? Patiently supportive is the phrase that comes to mind, but doesn't begin to give the picture.

Special thanks are due my editor, Marcia Marshall, for her enthusiasm and help in getting the warp and woof of the whole fabric in place.

B. S.

A mill girl standing beside a Fales & Jenks spinning frame. (A wood engraving from James Geldard's Handbook on Cotton Manufacture, 1867.)

Contents

II HARRIET HANSON ROBINSON
1825–1911

III SARAH G. BAGLEY
b. 1806

Brave New World

IN THE 1830s America was really two countries. If you ran two movies side by side, you would see first a life lived in the stark and simple ways of the early colonies. Memories of a hard-won revolution from the oppression of the British were still fresh. Snowbound in winter, working the soil and tending the livestock in the summer, a family was busy from dawn until nightfall. All its needs were provided right there in the home, or at someone's home nearby.

In the second film you would see a world catapulted into the modern age. And this was due mainly to the textile industry. On the banks of rivers and canals all over New England, factories were sprouting like mushrooms. Around these mills grew whole communities dedicated to this single occupation. A house was no longer something to be lived in for generations, but only a stopping-off place in a family's trek in search of work from one mill town to the next. The early spinning mills used child labor, and advertised without any shame for families with lots of offspring.

A view of Dutton Street showing the Merrimack mill (center) and boardinghouses (left). The wall of the canal supplying water power to the mills is beyond the trees (right).

Then, with the coming of the power loom for weaving, a device literally pirated from England by Francis Cabot Lowell, a new kind of work force was needed. What better choice than the young farm girl? Her father and brothers were busy on the land, or settling the western frontiers. Biding her time until marriage, she was isolated and bored, if she had any spirit. The few handicrafts available to her barely paid enough to live on.

"Daughters are now emphatically a blessing to the farmer," said one of the mill owners. Idleness was

4

considered a mortal sin in a world where there were not enough hands to do the work that was needed. The trick was to lure the young women to the city and overcome their families' fear that these would be pits of horror and depravity, as they saw the European model. The owners boasted about supervised boardinghouses for the virtuous, churches of every denomination for the pious, libraries for the literary, and enough shops to please any lady's fancy.

Lowell, to be called "The City of Spindles," was the second largest city in the country. By 1845, it had a population of thirty thousand, working in thirty-three mills, with over five hundred boardinghouses. Women in Lowell outnumbered men three to one. Each year the mills spewed out enough cloth to circle the globe two times over!

Years after the huge water wheels began powering the mills, the Lowell scene looked incredibly new and somewhat unreal. Charles Dickens, the world-famous British novelist, and one of the several famous people to visit this industrial showplace, said that it seemed to him as if "every 'Bakery,' 'Grocery' and 'Bookbindery' and every other kind of store, took its shutters down for the first time and started in business yesterday." And the mill girls amazed him. Unlike the brutalized and degraded mill operatives of England, these young people appeared well dressed, cheerful and brimming with intelligence. Many of the boardinghouses, he noticed, had pianos, and the lending libraries could scarcely supply the number of readers hungry for books.

But the greatest marvel of all was that they had begun publishing in 1840 a magazine called the *Lowell Offering* and all the writers were women working in the mills. Dickens later wrote: "I will only observe, putting out of sight the fact of the articles having been written by these girls after the arduous labors of the day, that it will compare advantageously with a great many English annuals."

A new girl arriving in Lowell would be no less startled than Dickens, but for her the shocks would be of a different order. Clutching a carpetbag or "hair trunk" of spotted calfskin and kicking up dust with every step along the treeless streets, she would arrive lonely and scared. The long rows of brick boarding-houses seemed like troops in an army. Soon she would be in a room with a half dozen other women, all seemingly chattering at once. They behaved as if they had been shut up in silence, which indeed they had, working anywhere from twelve to fourteen hours a day, depending on the season.

At precisely ten o'clock at night the boarding-house keeper, following the strict regulations set down by the company, would turn out the lights, and the talk would subside as the tired bodies sought needed rest.

The next day the new girl would be hired and conducted through the mill by the agent. The roar of the machinery was almost deafening. The girl would be a "spare hand" while one of the old-timers taught her the ropes. On payday it would all seem worthwhile, for the wage was in *cash* (most of the earlier spinning mills paid in "store orders" with goods available in the company store for credit—a kind of barter system always unfavorable to the employee). It was more money than she had held in her hand at any one time in her life.

In time, the country girl became a city girl. This was more than a change in outfit. It was a change in outlook. Soon, reading all the books, newspapers and magazines available, attending lyceum lectures and night classes, joining improvement circles and taking part in discussion on social issues, she became a woman of the world.

Conditions in the mills began to grow worse in the 1830s as the corporations chipped away at the wages and sped up the pace of work. All attempts to shorten the workday met with frustration. Workers in Lowell and other mill towns, most of them women, began to "turn out," or strike. Never before anywhere had women paraded down streets or spoken in public. Many of the newspapers called them upstarts and "Amazons," but this did not stop them.

In the 1840s, the Irish, escaping from the dread-

The Merrimack Corporation boardinghouse on Dutton Street just before their demolition. Photograph taken by Richard Graber in 1966.

ful "potato famine" at home, came in large numbers, followed by the Poles and French Canadians. Unlike the Yankee girls, these people could not "go home to Pa" when they were sick or tired out. They had no dreams of making more of their lives than being workers until the end. At first they lived in ill-ventilated and overcrowded hovels. Eventually they became a permanent factory population, coping much as the earlier generation had done.

The New England farm girls moved on. Some, used to putting their minds to work, entered "female seminaries," others went into new professions or settled the "wild west." Most married and transferred their skills to managing a home, which in that period was no easy matter. Mill girls were thought to make superior wives.

This book will focus on the lives of three women who lived in that unique time and place: Lucy Larcom, the most famous "graduate" of the mills, who got herself a belated education and became an innovating teacher, editor and popular poet; Harriet Hanson Robinson, a writer and outstanding figure in the long fight for woman's right to vote; and, finally, Sarah G. Bagley, fiery journalist, leader of the Female Labor Reform Association, whose presence flashed like a meteor across the Lowell horizon, to be lost to history thereafter.

If it had not been for their mill experience, these women might have languished unknown in the small rural towns from which they came. In their struggles they were enriched and enabled to become dynamic and ideal women of their time.

REGULATIONS

FOR THE

BOARDING HOUSES

OF THE

MIDDLESEX COMPANY.

THE tenants of the Boarding Houses are not to board, or permit any part of their houses to be occupied by any person except those in the employ of the Company.

They will be considered answerable for any improper conduct in their houses, and are not to permit their boarders to have company at unseasonable hours.

The doors must be closed at ten o'clock in the evening, and no one admitted after that time without some reasonable excuse.

The keepers of the Boarding Houses must give an account of the number, names, and employment of their boarders, when required; and report the names of such as are guilty of any improper conduct, or are not in the regular habit of attending public worship.

The buildings and yards about them must be kept clean and in good order, and if they are injured otherwise than from ordinary use, all necessary repairs will be made, and charged to the occupant.

It is indispensable that all persons in the employ of the Middlesex Company should be vaccinated who have not been, as also the families with whom they board; which will be done at the expense of the Company.

SAMUEL LAWRENCE, Agent.

JOEL TAYLOR, PRINTER, Daily Courier Office.

Boardinghouse regulations for the Middlesex Woolen Mills.

BOOK ONE

Lucy Larcom

1824 - 1893

1

Time Is Education

WHEN the stagecoach pulls up to the house they live in on Wallis Lane, it seems like a wonderful fantasy to Lucy, something out of an English storybook. She could count on the fingers of one hand the number of times she has been in a coach in her ten years of life. Only the three "babies" of the family will take this trip with their mother: Lydia, Octavia and herself.

Lucy watches the family belongings being piled onto a wagon which will follow behind them: chairs, tables, an old mahogany secretary with brass pulls, her mother's armchair. The chair had always seemed almost a part of her mother's body. Anyplace it traveled to had to be home. Lucy clutches a miniature picture of her father, painted on a sea voyage to Belgium, as if the strength of his spirit will help her now that he is no longer with them.

The town of Beverly never looked so beautiful: the quaint fishing boats on the wharf, the lighthouses a mile out blinking on and off, the church steeples of Danvers gleaming white in the distance. They cross the bridge to Salem, ride past miles of farm country, over gentle hills, until finally the largest city they have ever seen looms ahead.

The stagecoach leaves them on a long street with attached houses of sturdy red brick, with green doors and window shutters. These are the boardinghouses of the Lawrence Corporation. The mill itself can be seen down the street, an enormous structure with a bell tower, fronting on the river. Mrs. Larcom has been hired to run the house, and will be paid by the company with money taken from the mill girls' wages. It had been a difficult decision for her. In 1835, any mention of factories brought to mind the dingy, grimy mill towns of England. Mrs. Larcom had made a short visit to Lowell and so could reassure her worried relatives that the city would do them no harm. There were a lot of children to think about. The two oldest, daughters by a previous wife of Mr. Larcom's, were already married. But it was a wrench to leave five of her own children behind to work and live with other families. Still, as a widow, she was lucky to have any work at all.

A few days after they arrived, Lucy sat down and wrote a letter to her favorite sister Emeline: who, for the time, had remained in Beverly:

*The building that was Mrs. Larcom's boardinghouse
in the 1830s, owned by the Lawrence Corporation,
on Suffolk Street in Lowell.*

Dear Sister,
We have got a sink in our front entry. We
live in a three-story brick house with fourteen
doors on it. There is a canal close by. We ar-
rived safe after our fatiguing journey. We are
in good health and hope you are enjoying the
same blessing.

A tall, sturdy woman came several times a week
to help with the housework, but the three girls had to
do their stints, sewing and mending linens, doing er-
rands, washing dishes. Octavia, aged eight, was so
small she had to stand on a "cricket" to reach the high
sink.

Most of the boarders were from distant states
like Vermont, New Hampshire and Maine. Some had
odd-sounding and romantic names—Zilpha, Kezia,
Rosanna, and even one Lovey. Many spoke with the
"downeast" dialect, a combination of the Scotch and
Irish of their ancestors with a Yankee twang. They
said "daown" and "haow." When Lucy began telling
one of them about how once, when her brother went
to sea, the ship was set afire and robbed by some free-
booters, the girl looked a bit disdainful. "They don't
think much of sailors up *aour* way," she said.

The girls would burst into the dining room for
their meals and talk as fast as they could between
bites. The meal breaks were only a half hour long,

and they had to come from the mill and return to it in that time. Evening suppers were more leisurely. Lucy found out a great deal about the lives of the operatives at that hour. Each one seemed to have come to Lowell for a different reason. One was there because her parents were invalids and she was helping to pay the mortgage on the family home; another had been bored in her tiny village and had heard that Lowell had circulating libraries and lyceum lectures; a third came to save for her marriage dowry while her boyfriend was off on a long whaling voyage; another wanted to be able to afford the kind of fashions women were wearing in Boston; still another to keep an eye on her fiancé who worked in a mill where there were three times as many women as men.

Some were there to save up for their own schooling, but even more were putting their brothers through college. It was said that a quarter of the men attending Harvard were put through by the sacrifices made by working sisters.

There was not much leisure time left after the thirteen-hour workday. In the few hours between supper and the ten o'clock curfew, there was the sewing of new clothes and repairing of old ones, books and magazines to read, letters to be written. Those who did not go "out upon the street" often gathered in some common room—sometimes it was the dining room—after the chairs had been taken away.

Peddlers came almost every night, selling candy, perfume, shoes, books, or tickets to some event. To some girls these men were an annoyance, to others a butt for teasing. A piece in the *Lowell Offering* described a man pretending to be a "professor," dressed in a long frock coat. He was trying to induce the women to come and see a show of "pictures":

> *"Now ladies," said he, showing his teeth and rubbing his hands together, and then wringing them and twisting them all manner of ways. "Only two shillings for a ticket. You'll see things you never saw in your life before: Little insects magnified as big as a hoss. You'll see the sun to be inhabited jest like this earth, folks, there fifty miles high—and the spots, them are the shadders."*

Silly fads and serious ideas got equal attention in the boardinghouses. "Phrenologists" came and placed their hands on the girls' heads, feeling for the bumps, and providing character "readings." A visit from a hypnotist would start a trend, with each one looking for another to use as a "subject." Vegetarianism was popular after a certain Professor Graham (after whom the graham cracker was named) warned against eating "anything that had life in it." Millerites gloomily predicted the end of the world and told the

Lucy's mother, Lois Larcom.

girls they had better prepare their souls for eternity. Everyone talked about Brook Farm, a socialist community, where mental and physical labor were considered equally valuable.

Mrs. Larcom was generous and spent every penny she was paid and more to see that her boarders were comfortable and well fed. Before the family had been there a year though, she realized that she could not manage unless one of the children worked. At the time Lucy and Lydia were the oldest ones with her. They were eleven and thirteen. Mrs. Larcom took them both to see the agent at the Lawrence mill. He had a room of his own in the counting house, a small building near the mill. There was just one opening, he said, for a "doffer" or "bobbin girl" in the spinning room. This was the only job available to children and was very easy, he assured them. Of course, the corporation would honor the law that had just been passed in the state legislature, requiring that all persons under fifteen be taken out of the mill for schooling three months out of every year. Since Lucy was taller than Lydia, the agent took her for the older one and told her she was hired. She was ecstatic at the chance to help the family.

Once inside the mill, the volume of noise was overwhelming. One had to talk loudly right into someone's ear to be heard at all. Although the spinning room was not quite as noisy as the weave room, it was still a little frightening to see the rows and rows of spindles whizzing continuously as they took the loose cotton fibers and twisted them into thread. When the bobbins inside the spindles became filled with the newly spun thread, the doffers replaced them with empty ones. The bobbin boxes carried by the doffers were bigger than they were.

The doffing took about fifteen minutes and had to be done once an hour. The rest of the time the children could read, play, or run home to the boardinghouse for a snack. The spinners all were friendly and sometimes took a few of the children aside to sing with them or have them recite poetry or parts of the catechism. There was a fascinating older woman who worked as a sweeper in the room. She had just fled from Ireland, where the potato famine was causing mass starvation, and had many tales to tell about "the ould counthry."

At first the work seemed more like fun than anything else. "Why, it's nothing but a game," she told her mother, who had felt somewhat guilty at having to send her out to earn a living so young. But as the weeks and months went on, the days seemed longer and longer. In a long narrative poem about Lowell, called *An Idyl of Work*, Lucy would write:

> *When I first*
> *Learned to doff bobbins, I just thought it play,*
> *But when you do the same thing twenty times—*
> *A hundred times a day—it is so dull!*

In spite of the monotony, the children found it thrilling seeing how the dirty puffs of cotton received by the mill in huge bales could be converted into the sleek yards of cotton sheeting and pretty calico prints.

Design for a five dollar bill to be issued by a Lowell bank, 1860, showing doffers at work.

They were allowed to watch the enormous water wheel through a trapdoor on the lowest floor. The turning of the wheel to supply the power for all the machinery made Lucy think of the God who set the universe into motion.

The bales of cotton were brought into a picking house close to the mills, where the coarse fluff was separated into loose fibers and the dirt removed. Next, in the carding room of the mill these "laps" went through machines that combed and drew them into thinner fibers called "roving." In the spinning room on the second floor, where Lucy worked, long rows of spindles turned the roving into yarn suitable for weaving. Some of the yarn was taken to the dressing room where it was "dressed" or starched to make it firm enough to serve as the warp of the looms.

The power looms in the weave room wove the yarn into cloth. Energetic operatives preferred being weavers because they got paid by the piece and could earn sometimes twice as much as the other workers. In the cloth room the finished fabric got measured, folded and separated into piles to be dyed, bleached or sent out for sale.

During her first school break, Lucy had a sadistic teacher named Master Hill. Once when a boy played a prank on another with a straight pin, the teacher chased the boy around the room trying to stick a pin in his shoulder. Lucy, as always, had difficulty with arithmetic, but rather than get help from the teacher, she allowed another schoolmate to do her sums for her.

However, the second time around, the whole system in the public school had been changed. The teachers were kind and taught well. In those three months Lucy learned more than she had in all her years of earlier schooling. When she was told she was ready for high school, she was thrilled. More than anything else in life she wanted to *learn*. But this was not to be.

> *The little money I could earn—one dollar a week, besides the price of my board—was needed in the family, and I must return to the mill. It was a severe disappointment to me, though I did not say so at home.*

Lucy heard a neighbor saying to Mrs. Larcom that while *his* daughter needed to go to high school, hers did not. "My girl hasn't got such a head-piece as yours has," he said. Lucy would always remember that remark.

At fourteen Lucy was as tall as a grown woman. Her sisters insisted that she be made "seeable." They took her mass of curly brown hair and twisted it into a bun on the top of her head. Into this neat coil they popped in a tortoise shell comb, then fashionable

Lucy as a young woman.

among the women. She took growing up very seriously. Harriet Hanson and Lucy had met as doffers, and Harriet carried into later life an image of Lucy strolling across a bridge at a narrow part of the Merrimack River.

I passed her, a tall and bonnie young girl, with her head in the clouds. After a little nod of recognition, as I looked up at her—for although she was only a year older than I, she was much larger and more mature—she went on. But to me she seemed so grand, so full of thought, that, with girlish admiration I forgot my errand, turned, stood still, and thoughtfully watched her out of sight.

Lucy had four jobs in the course of her ten years in the mills. She went from doffer to spinner, disliking both because of the noise and dust. Her third job was in the dressing room, working alongside of her beloved older sister Emeline, who had just come to Lowell to join the family. Lucy had no love of machinery but the whirling spindles at least had been manageable. She thought the dressing frame behaved like a brat. "It had to be watched in a dozen directions every minute, and even then it was always getting itself and me into trouble." It was a creature beyond her control. Before long she found herself inquiring about a place in the cloth room. It was the lowest paid work of all, but it was quiet and clean, and best of all, it was said that the women were allowed to read there while waiting for deliveries of finished cloth.

When she signed out of the dressing room the paymaster asked her if she was going where she could earn more money.

"No," she said, "I'm going where I can have more time."

"Ah, yes," the man said, looking wise. "Time *is* money, isn't it?"

"No," Lucy answered quietly, "time is education."

2

Fame

THE cloth room was in a long, low brick building. The cloth was pressed by a hydraulic machine and then measured. The pressing was generally done by men. Women measured and folded the bolts of cloth and recorded the statistics into a ledger. Lucy found she could read whole books during breaks in the work and even jot down snatches of poetry that came to mind. There was a lot of good feeling among the workers in this room, perhaps because they had more time to get to know each other. They were called "the cloth room aristocracy" because of the shorter hours and the fact that they could wear street clothes without work aprons. Sometimes in the summer the girls would wear white dresses, unheard of in the rest of the mill.

The Superintendent of the Lawrence Corporation was a tall, dignified man who liked to wander through the rooms to see how things were going. One day, as Lucy was poring over an eighteenth-century religious book, Cotton Mather's *Magnalia Christi Americana*, she was startled to see the man peering over her shoulder to see what she was reading. His only comment was, "A valuable old book, that!"

To be found with a book in any other part of the mill was to bring on the wrath of an overseer. Books were hidden in apron pockets or in wastebaskets. Sometimes they were torn apart and read page by page. When Lucy was a spinner she had pasted clippings of poems on the window frames. Other spinners called them "Lucy's window gems" and some of them imitated her. The overseers varied in severity. Some would overlook the books they saw protruding out of garments, while others would snatch them away. One overseer confiscated all the Bibles he could find. Once he snapped to one of the most religious girls in the mill, "I did think you had more conscience than to bring that book here!"

When Lucy was working in the spinning room, a relative asked her, "How can you think with all that noise?" "How can anyone live *without* thinking," was Lucy's answer.

Lucy's thinking usually involved forming rhymes. In her childhood she had been considered a genius in the family, asked to recite aloud from the age of seven. Once someone told her mother, "Keep what Lucy writes till she grows up. I have heard of somebody who earned a thousand dollars by writing poetry!"

There was a whole network of evening classes in Lowell. When a few girls found enough interest in a particular subject, one of them would search out an expert to teach it. Notices were posted on the mill gates and drew large numbers of operatives.

The typical charge for a class was one dollar for twelve sessions, or half a week's pay.

Lucy took a botany course with Frances Whipple Green. Green had already achieved some fame with a novel about a worker's life. She had also edited a labor paper, the *Wampanoag and Operatives' Journal*. Under its masthead had been the motto: "Idleness and luxury pamper the *animal*—labor makes the *man*." In Lowell, Green was assembling material for a botany textbook. The course included rambles in the fields around Lowell to examine species of flowers. For this a girl had to find a "spare hand" who would do her work.

A German class was held in a boardinghouse that had a fancy parlor with bookshelves along the wall. Lucy struggled with the difficult guttural sounds and odd Gothic lettering. At the end of each class the German teacher would bring out his guitar and sing songs of his native land. He got Lucy to translate a few and they were issued as sheet music. Some German poets were writing in a style that was half essay. Lucy experimented with this prose-poem form. Her first book would be a collection of them.

B. C. SARGEANT,
BOOKSELLER AND STATIONER,
CITY HALL BUILDING, LOWELL.

*An advertisement showing Lowell's City Hall in the
1840s. Lyceum lectures were held on the second story.*

Everyone looked forward to Wednesdays. On
that evening the operatives could get out of work a bit
earlier to attend the Lowell Lyceum lectures held in a
huge room at the Town Hall. New England's most
interesting intellectuals came to lecture there. One of
them was Ralph Waldo Emerson, the poet and philosopher, who charmed everyone with his soft, melodi-

ous voice and startling ideas. The philosophy he propagated was called Transcendentalism. As Lucy later wrote:

> *A bewildered discussion followed as to whether we had understood, or only imagined we understood, what the lecture was about. We were sure we had a glimpse of something grand beyond us, though nobody could tell exactly what.*

In some cities the women who attended lectures had to come with a male sponsor. Harriet Robinson reported that "it was thought almost disgraceful for women to go to a public meeting without male protection, and they went with veiled faces, as if ashamed to be seen of man."

In Lowell no faces were veiled. The women comprised more than half of every audience. Sitting politely through the band music that preceded each lecture, they would pull out note paper as soon as the speaker began. A visiting Harvard professor claimed that he had never seen "so assiduous note-taking, no, not even in a college class."

Lucy's sister Emeline was a special sort of person. In Beverly, when Mrs. Larcom had been suddenly widowed and the large family had become too much for her, Emeline was a second mother to the younger children. Once she promised them she would remain "an old maid" forever and keep taking care of them. In Lowell she was everyone's mother. When someone was ill, Emeline was immediately at her side. She gave most of her wages to charity, allowing herself only one going-out dress, a Merrimack print. She said that having only one always simplified her choices. When the young people in the boardinghouse came in shivering and complaining about the winter frost, she would say, "But it doesn't make you any warmer to *say* you are cold." She herself took a bath every morning in a large basin of cold water in which, often, pieces of ice were floating.

Emeline was concerned that the young ones not be "mentally defrauded" by having had to go to work so young. And so one day she suggested that a few relatives and friends meet to talk about a home newspaper. They met in the attic of Mrs. Larcom's boardinghouse on a Saturday when the mills closed early.

The handwritten newspapers went through several evolutions. The first version was called *The Casket*, the second *The Bouquet*, the final and longest-lasting one, *The Diving Bell*. The first number had a lead poem by Emeline:

> *Our diving bell shall deep descend*
> *And bring from the immortal mind*
> *Thoughts that to improve us tend*
> *Of each variety and kind.*

Also on the subject of the mind was an essay by Lucy, then fourteen:

> *What a beaufiful and noble thing is mind. It is the great principle of action. The smallest, and most trifling things we do are suggested by our minds. Without it we would be on a level with brute creation. We should store our minds with wisdom and useful knowledge and in due time they will unfold greater beauties than those of face and form.*

One day as Emeline was leaving the mill she was approached by Harriot Curtis, a literary woman who worked by her side. Harriot said that some of the women she knew had heard about the attic meetings and wanted to form a "society for mutual improvement." Shortly afterward, a small group of women got together. Curtis made an inspiring speech about how important it was for working women to use their intellects, but when officers were chosen, she modestly declined. Emeline was made secretary.

This Improvement Circle meeting in 1837 was the first recorded literary club of women. The idea spread, and by the middle of the following decade there were seven circles in various parts of the city. The most successful one was connected with the Universalist Church, where Rev. Abel Thomas presided over the "intellectual banquets," as he called them.

Harriet Farley, who was to become an editor of the mill girls' publication, wrote about these early meetings:

> *The gentlemen were at liberty to contribute to the Circle, but they were of no great assistance. It was soon found that the principal interest of the meetings depended upon the* factory girls. *There were so many articles that it was thought they might form a pleasing variety in a little book.*

The "little book" was to be called *Garland of the Mills* and to be fashioned after the gift annuals so popular at the time. Then Reverend Thomas had an inspiration. Why not a magazine?

An experimental issue with a bright yellow cover appeared October, 1840. It was called the *Lowell Offering: a Repository of Original Articles, Written by Females Actively Employed in the Mills.* The girls were almost as excited by this venture as the readers. "We had seen or heard the articles before," one of them wrote, "but they seemed so much better in print! They sounded as if written by people who never worked at all!"

For the first two years Reverend Thomas served as editor. From 1842, Harriet Farley and Harriot

LOWELL

OFFERING

December, 1845.

" Is Saul also among the prophets."

A REPOSITORY

OF ORIGINAL ARTICLES, WRITTEN BY

"FACTORY GIRLS."

LOWELL: MISSES CURTIS & FARLEY.
BOSTON: JORDAN & WILEY, 121
Washington street.
1845.

Curtis shared the editorship. William Schouler, owner of the *Lowell Courier,* a somewhat conservative newspaper in the town, provided financial backing for the early years of the publication. Farley, coming from an extremely impoverished family, had worked at traditional women's trades from the age of fourteen. At Lowell, she earned enough to help support her large family. Curtis, born in a small hamlet in Vermont, was determined to find a way to educate herself. She had already published a popular novel, *Kate in Search of a Husband,* and would be starting another one in the pages of the *Offering.*

The magazine was a mild sensation, and by the fifth issue it became a regular monthly, receiving the official support of Lowell's notable citizens, among them several superintendents of the corporations. It was no surprise when Schouler's newspaper praised the *Offering,* but when reviews started coming in from other parts of the country and even from overseas, the girls were overwhelmed.

Cover of the Lowell Offering *(last issue), described by the magazine as "the New England school-girl, of which our factories are made up, standing near a beehive, emblem of industry and intelligence, and in the background the Yankee schoolhouse, church and factory."*

Harriet Martineau, the English economist, had been to Waltham where Francis Cabot Lowell had set up the first mills. Like Charles Dickens, she was so struck by the contrast between the American mills and the British, she was lavish in her praise. In 1843, after receiving leather-bound volumes of the *Offering* as a gift from three Harriets on the staff, she sat down and wrote a letter of thanks, which was published in the magazine. "It is a welcome token of kindness, and for its own value, and above all as a proof of sympathy between you and me, in regard to that great subject, the true honor and interests of our sex." She appealed to the American operatives to fight against the tariff that prevented British manufactures from coming into the country. She begged them to think of the "scrambling of the starving for work at any price, of the English operatives who lead lives of shame, and blindness, and death before the age of twenty-five." Martineau sent the volumes to the London Athenaeum Club's library, hoping that Queen Victoria would take note that women working under more humane conditions could accomplish so amazing a feat. Martineau had a collection of *Offering* pieces published in England, calling the book *Mind Among the Spindles*.

One short-lived competitor of the *Offering* was *Operatives' Magazine*. This was issued by the improvement circle at the Congregational Church, to which Lucy and Emeline belonged. Reverend Amos Blanchard, a friendly and fatherly man, was in charge of the circle and the magazine was edited by two women who had left the mills to teach school. It had a religious tone and was informally called "the orthodox magazine." Among the many pieces of Lucy's to be published in it was a sentimental poem about her lost childhood. She was seventeen when she wrote:

> *My childhood! O those pleasant days, when*
> *   everything seemed free,*
> *And in the broad and verdant fields I frol-*
> *   icked merrily;*
> *When joy came to my bounding heart with*
> *   every wild bird's song,*
> *And Nature's music in my ears was ringing all*
> *   day long!*

The *Operatives' Magazine* merged into the *Offering* in 1842, and Lucy became a regular contributor and the one who was to be its most famous alumna.

It was a day long remembered when *Offering* editor Harriet Farley brought the poet John Greenleaf Whittier, a neighbor of hers from Amesbury, to a circle meeting. It was a warm evening and the girls looked particularly pretty in their light-colored dresses. Whittier's antislavery poetry had been passed from hand to hand in the mills, so the group was thrilled to see him in person. Lucy got up and read a poem called "Sabbath Bells."

> Now the mellow light has gone,
> And the gentle stars look down
> Through the darkened sky aloft
> And the moonbeams, still and soft,
> Fall on the tree, and dale and hill.
> All is peaceful, solemn, still.
> 'Tis the knell of holy time,
> And the spirit upward swells
> With the Sabbath evening bells.

When the handsome poet came over to congratulate Lucy on her work, she was so embarrassed she started to hide behind a friend. But the few words they exchanged was the beginning of a friendship to last both their lifetimes.

The writing in the *Offering* tended to be the sentimental poetry and fanciful stories then popular, but people also wanted to know what it felt like to be working in this supposed industrial paradise.

Reading the *Offering* with its tiny eye-wrenching type, we do get a vivid picture of the mill girls' lives. We see the newcomer getting accustomed with difficulty to the confusing and demanding machinery. There are the hurried meals with scarcely time to "masticate" the food. Then the joys of leisure time, reading, socializing, patronizing the shops of every description created to tap this enormous buying public. Sundays are days of rest but also of compulsory church attendance, which the girls transform into fashion shows. There is so much religious proselytizing that sometimes the religious tracts are trampled underfoot, there are so many of them. The boardinghouses are homes away from home. The keepers are sympathetic listeners to the girls' troubles, whether they be due to lost lovers or aching teeth. In the boardinghouses ideas are exchanged and complaints are aired. This closeness, which grows between roommates and workmates, makes it easier to join together to improve conditions.

On this question the *Offering* balanced on a precarious tightrope, with the "spirit of discontent," on the one hand, and editor Farley's fear of confronting the corporations. In the third volume she expressed her feelings about the role of the magazine in the operatives' lives:

> *We should like to influence them as moral and rational beings—to point out their duties to themselves, and to each other. Our field is a wide one, though many subjects are excluded. With wages, board, etc. we have nothing to do—these depend on circumstances over which we have no control.*

By the 1840s, "wages" and "board" were very much
on people's minds, since the prosperity of the industry
was not showing either in the wage or the conditions
of work. Because the *Offering* was losing its readers to
the more political publications like the *Voice of Industry*, it went under in 1845, to emerge three years
later briefly as the *New England Offering*. This magazine was not the kind of cooperative effort the old one
had been. Farley wrote to Harriet Robinson:

> *I do all the publishing, editing, canvassing;
> and as it is bound in my office, I can, in a
> hurry help fold, cut covers, stitch, etc.*

The truth was that the kind of readers the magazines had attracted were leaving the city in great
numbers. The Yankee farm girl, who had come seek-
ing independence, found her situation more and more
degraded.

Other kinds of work were opening up to women.
It was said that ten thousand girls from mill towns
journeyed west to settle, many of them becoming
schoolteachers. Their places were taken by immi-
grants from Europe and Canada.

In 1846, Emeline, now married, decided to
move out West with the family, and Lucy became a
member of this party of five adults and one baby,
Emeline's, to make the long trek. The Improvement

Circle made a surprise farewell party for her. She almost dissolved into tears as gift after gift was presented. The editors of the *Offering* gave her twenty dollars, telling her it was in payment for her contributions. As Lucy recalled:

> *I said positively that I should return soon,*
> *but underneath my protestations I was afraid*
> *that I might not. The West was very far off*
> *then—a full week's journey. It would be hard*
> *getting back. Those I loved might die; I*
> *might die myself.*

In spite of these morbid thoughts, Lucy managed to be cheerful as she made preparations to leave the city where she had spent all her growing years. She was twenty-two. It was time to explore another kind of life.

3

Love on the Prairie

LUCY keeps a diary on the voyage West by steamboat, railroad and stagecoach. At one point she writes:

> Came on the steamboat "Worcester" in darkness. And here we are, three of us, squeezed into the queerest little cubby-hole of a state-room that could be thought of. We all sat down on the floor and laughed till we cried, to see ourselves in such close companionship! We had a dispute, just for the fun of it, as to who should occupy the highest shelf. I painted the catastrophe that would occur, should I come down with my full weight upon the rest, in such glowing colors, that they were willing to consign me to the second shelf.

They go along Long Island Sound, then down the Delaware River, seeing new countryside passing like a panorama. Lucy begins to feel homesick, but soon is distracted by having to tend all the others who are terribly seasick. In a stagecoach crossing the Allegheny mountains nine adults and the baby are squeezed in with almost no air to breathe. The baby cries and the other riders complain about the baby. Lucy wishes she were a baby herself, so she could cry.

Finally the group arrived at Looking Glass Prairie in Illinois. There were six in the household: Lucy, Sarah, a friend from Lowell, Emeline, her husband George Spaulding, their baby George-Francis, and, finally, George's brother Frank, who was born exactly the same month as Lucy. Emeline had previously lost one child, and she doted on this little boy, who was, very shortly, to go the way of the first. Infant mortality was very high in the nineteenth century. Of Emeline's twelve children, only six survived into adulthood.

The cabin they were to share was rustic. Planks resting on bricks had to serve as a couch, curtains as doors. Outside it was one expanse of grass as far as the eye could see. The closest neighbor was so far away that the house looked like a piece of wood placed endwise.

Lucy began to teach in primitive log cabin

Lucy's favorite sister, Emeline.

schools. She would walk over prairie miles to get to work, with only the "cattle brutes" for company. The "young ideas" she taught were not very sophisticated. And whatever any of them brought in for textbooks had to serve.

In one school a boy disappeared up a chimney when Lucy wasn't looking, and after a frantic search, was found in back of the school dancing a little jig. Another mite sat with his feet dangling on benches reserved for older children. He said he'd "heap rather sit with the big fellers." Lucy could get no name out of him but "Bub." A girl when asked her age said, "Gosh, I dunno. Never was inside a schoolhouse before!"

Lucy went from school to school, working at each a few months. She was generally hired by a committee of parents, who begrudged her the forty dollars they paid her for three months' work.

Eventually George Spaulding became a minister and the family moved to Woodburn, a more "Yankified" town, where Lucy taught in a comfortable white schoolhouse with no cracks in the floors or walls, and real windows.

Whenever Emeline was sick, Lucy had to take over the housework: cooking, baking, sewing, churning butter, making candles, plus watching the young ones. She realized for the first time how burdensome a married woman's life could be. She wrote to a friend, "O the misery of having memory, thought, and invention continually tasked over beef, bread-and-butter, coffee, mops, brooms and soapsuds!" They had a saying on the frontier: *this is a fine country for men and dogs, but women and oxen have to take it!*

Frank Spaulding, George's younger brother, was becoming restless. Back East he had worked at a variety of jobs, being unable to settle at any one. He had been a fabrics salesman, a bookkeeper, he had fished in the Merrimack, chopped wood and peddled milk. Now, in Illinois, he was a teacher, but felt his destiny lay elsewhere. When wagons began to pass across the plains on their way to the west coast, he decided to join them. The "California fever" was on, after gold was discovered in the Sierra Nevada mountains. Frank thought that on this furthest frontier he might find a niche for himself, which proved to be true. There was only one problem: Frank and Lucy had fallen in love.

Lucy did not want him to leave. She told him that if he left her now, she would consider him as if dead. By 1850, however, Frank was in San Francisco, sending Lucy specimens of "yellow dirt" to be made into jewelry. He was beginning to learn about practicing medicine. He wrote long letters asking her to join him, telling her how much he longed to be with her.

The correspondence went on for years. Reading Lucy's letters one sees how her feelings changed as time passed. *Whenever I think of Frank, my heart goes out to him with such a longing desire to comfort and help, that I could almost believe I love him enough to go to him at once. . . .*

I am afraid I should not make him happy, and for several reasons I should prefer passing my life in single blessedness. . . .

If I lay down my arms and begin to live for comfort and pleasure, I must expect discontent and sadness. . . .

I am getting cool about emigrating to the golden land. . . .

My heart is strangely asleep.

Whether she was conscious of it or not, Lucy was making a choice facing other women of her time: to get married and live a life of continuous domestic toil, or to be an independent woman with the time and energy to pursue a creative life. When she was only in her thirties, she began to refer to herself as "an old maid" and to prepare herself for her calling: to be a writer. But Frank and Lucy continued the correspondence, she merely to be friendly, he clinging to the hope that she would say "yes" finally.

One of the new "female seminaries" was located at Alton, Illinois, not far from where Lucy was teaching school. In 1849, she was persuaded by friends to talk to the Principal of Monticello Seminary, Philena Fobes. Lucy was most impressed by Miss Fobes, who seemed to combine an enormous knowledge with a sweetness of character. Although at twenty-five Lucy was a decade older than most of the students, she enrolled at the Seminary. As a kind of scholarship, she taught primary classes at first, and then was put in charge of Monticello's Preparatory School, for children under fourteen.

The school did not place the heavy emphasis on "domestic economy" that was fashionable in the seminaries of the East. The courses resembled the men's colleges of the day, from which females were excluded. The greatest difference between them was that boys entering places like Harvard and Yale had to show a thorough knowledge of Latin and Greek, translating to those languages from English and from them to English.

One of the special features of Monticello was the public graduation ceremony in which girls of all classes displayed their learning and talents. There was no other institution like it west of the Mississippi.

Lucy was remembered most for her warmth and gentleness. One of her students told Miss Fobes, "Miss Larcom is such a lovely teacher! She told us today we must move the chairs gently, as if they had feelings." One of her colleagues remembered later that after arriving at Monticello for the first time, feeling very much like a stranger, she was suddenly greeted by "a large fair-faced woman, and looked up to meet a pair of happy eyes smiling down at me, so full of sweet human kindness that the dark clouds fell straight away."

After completing the three-year course of study at Monticello, Lucy returned East to become a teacher at what would later be Wheaton College in Norton, Massachusetts. Here she taught history, literature, moral philosophy and composition. It was she who introduced English literature as a separate study in the seminary's curriculum. Most teachers followed their textbooks pretty closely in class, but Lucy instead introduced a lot of free discussion. Students who had not prepared their lessons well would sometimes take advantage of this and prolong the discussion endlessly so that Lucy could not proceed to the next topic. She took it all in good grace. In the tradition of the improvement circles and mill girl magazines, she started a literary society and two magazines, the *Chrysalis* and the *Rushlight* for the lower and upper grades. All three were in existence a century later.

Every afternoon Wheaton Seminary had something they called General Exercises in which worthy compositions were read, newspaper items were talked about and songs were sung. One day, in 1855, a group of students prepared a surprise for Lucy. As the piano banged out the accompaniment to the folksong "Nelly Bly," they sang:

> *Yeomen strong, hither throng!*
> *Nature's honest men,*
> *We will make the wilderness*
> *Bud and bloom again,*
> *Bring the sickle, speed the plough,*
> *Turn the ready soil!*
> *Freedom is the noblest pay*
> *For the true man's toil.*
> *Ho! brothers! come brothers!*
> *Hasten all with me,*
> *We'll sing upon the Kanzas plains*
> *A song of liberty!*

Lucy was so startled she cried out and buried her face in her hands. She had written the song and won a nationwide contest, but had not heard the news. The father of one of the Wheaton girls had mailed the newspaper clipping containing the verses to his daughter. Lucy's prize was fifty dollars. Her winning song would be reprinted many times and sung all over the country. It was even printed on cotton kerchiefs that were distributed by the thousands.

In 1855, the United States Congress had passed the Kansas-Nebraska Act, which allowed states west of Missouri, previously forbidden to become slave states, to decide for themselves. That meant that new states like Kansas would become battlegrounds for slave interests against northern antislavery people. A New England Emigrant Aid Company was set up to encourage the settling of Kansas by abolitionists or sympathizers. In the long run they were successful, beating out the wealthy southerners, who couldn't get enough support to do the same. Lucy's song, "Call to Kanzas" was an inspiration to the new settlers.

Also in 1855, Lucy's first book was published, consisting of prose-poems, some of which had appeared in the *Offering*. It was called *Similitudes* and was issued in decorative editions, suitable for gift giving. In 1858, *Lottie's Thought Book* was issued by the American Sunday School Union, the first of several books by Lucy written for the child reader.

At the same time, Lucy had been submitting poetry to many newspapers and magazines and was beginning to get a small income from her writing. One of her poems caused something of a scandal, and as a result both the poem and the poet became well known to the public.

The poem, "Hannah Binding Shoes," had been sent to a magazine called the *Knickerbocker*. More than a year passed and Lucy got no response from them whatever, so she sent it to the *Crayon*. When it was published there, a letter appeared in the *New York Tribune* accusing Lucy of being a "literary thiefess." The *Knickerbocker* had, apparently, published the poem with a fictitious author's name and forgotten that Lucy had sent it. Lucy wrote to the *Tribune* setting the records straight and wrote a nasty letter to the *Knickerbocker*. "Hannah Binding Shoes" was read and recited and set to music by more than one composer.

Lucy had once seen a woman's face at a window in her native town of Beverly, and the face had haunted her for years because it seemed to speak of the terrible tragedies of ships lost at sea. Here, in the poem, a young woman grows old waiting for a husband who will never return.

> *Twenty winters*
> *Bleach and tear the ragged shore she views.*
> *Twenty seasons:*
> *Never one has brought her any news.*
> *Still her dim eyes silently*

Chase the white sails o'er the sea:
Hopeless, faithful,
Hannah's at the window binding shoes.

Lucy had renewed her friendship with John Greenleaf Whittier upon her return east. She became a regular visitor in the Amesbury house where Whittier, or "Greenleaf," as his friends called him, lived with his sister Elizabeth. Elizabeth developed a strong attachment to Lucy, with whom she found "more rest and trust" than with almost any other soul. Whittier and Lucy exchanged many letters about the growing conflict on the issue of slavery. Both were shaken by the execution of John Brown.

Lucy wrote to Harriet Robinson, "John Brown is to be hung tomorrow. Do we live in Christiandom? I think America needs missionaries from some more enlightened land."

When the Civil War began, Lucy had a pang in her heart seeing the young men from Beverly parading off to battle down the streets of Boston. Riding back and forth from Norton to Boston she observed an army camp and its "long array of white tents, the soldiers marching and countermarching, and the hills tinted with sunset and autumn at once, looking down upon the camping ground."

Some of the girls at Wheaton were from the South, and a few wore emblems representing the slave states. The northern girls cut them cold and there was a lot of tension in the air. Lucy resolved the situation by suggesting that people do something rather than talk. Students and teachers began knitting socks and sewing shirts for the Union army. Some girls wrote letters to the men at the front, stuffing them into the pockets of the shirts. "We are living in a grand time now," Whittier wrote to Lucy. "One year now is worth a dozen of the years of our ancestors."

As the relationship between Lucy and Frank Spaulding faded away, Lucy heard that Frank's sympathies were with the South. Eventually he married a woman who was the niece of one of the governors of South Carolina. Her feelings about the ending of their friendship and her loyalty to the antislavery cause resulted in a poem called "A Loyal Woman's No!" It was published in the *Atlantic Monthly* and was widely read and talked about. "How much we like thy 'A Loyal Woman's No!' " Whittier wrote to her. "I see it as immensely popular—a proof that people regard it as a 'a word in season.' "

When the agonizing war was finally over, Whittier wrote the poem "Laus Deo" describing the jubilant celebration in Amesbury where he lived.

Ring, O bells!
Every stroke exulting tells
Of the burial hour of crime.

Loud and long, that all might hear,
Ring for every listening ear
Of Eternity and Time!

This time it was Lucy who congratulated the poet. Whittier wrote to her describing how the poem had written itself in his head as he sat in Quaker meeting. "I am glad they liked my poem in the *Independent.* It wrote itself, or rather sang itself, while the bells rang."

In 1862, after eight years at Wheaton Seminary, Lucy left, to return many times as a friend of the institution. She had mixed feelings about teaching. On the one hand she loved to see how the young women blossomed under her guidance, but since her days in the Lowell boardinghouses, she had developed a fierce dislike of sharing her living quarters with others. "So many cold, dismal hours as I have had, shivering in the midst of a multitude," she had written to one of her friends. Now she heard the call of her poetic muse and realized that she might make a modest living as a writer.

A special issue of Wheaton's the *Rushlight* was issued in 1894 as a tribute to the illustrious teacher who was to be one of New England's most popular and beloved of poets. It is one of the warmest accounts of Lucy's life, particularly her middle years.

4

Whittier: Friend to Woman

EIGHTEEN sixty-five was to be a banner year for Greenleaf Whittier. As a young abolitionist journalist he had been attacked by vicious mobs and had his newspaper, the *Pennsylvania Freeman*, set afire along with Pennsylvania Hall, which had just been built by a group of reformers. Now when his cause was everyone's cause and the war had been fought and won, Whittier rose to fame quickly.

He wrote a long poem based on his own family's life in rural New England and sent it to his publisher James T. Fields. He wrote to Lucy: "I wanted to send my manuscript of *Snow-Bound*, but was sick and the poem was in fragments. I *have* sent it, however, to Fields, and he likes it so much that he means to make a book of it. It is a winter idyl—a picture of an old-fashioned farmer's fireside in winter—and if it were not mine I should call it pretty good."

The book was an instant best-seller. The first printing sold at a rate of a thousand copies a day. "We can't keep the plaguey thing quiet," Fields wrote to him. "I fear it will be impossible to get along without printing another batch!"

Whittier became not only famous but wealthy as a result of the book. He made ten thousand dollars in royalties, which was an enormous sum at that time.

But success did not spoil him. He was essentially a shy person, who morbidly hid away from crowds and adulation. Toward other writers he was always supportive. Women writers in particular owed whatever success they achieved to Whittier, who gave them helpful criticism and solicited publishers for them. For Lucy he served as a mentor as well as a friend, starting very early in her career.

Shortly after she left the mills, Whittier had published Lucy's poetry in the *National Era*, an antislavery newspaper he helped edit. He asked his readers to note that the verses were written "by a young woman whose life has been no long holyday of leisure, but one of toil and privation."

He sent the manuscript of her first book to his publisher saying that it was "unique and beautiful" and "exactly the thing for publication." For a number of years he tried to get a collection of hers published, and in 1869, when Fields finally issued her *Poems*, Whittier wrote a lengthy "estimate" which served as an advertisement:

Its author holds in rare combination the healthfulness of simple truth and common sense, with a fine and delicate fancy, and an artist's perception of all beauty. Her ballads have the true flavor and feeling of the breezy New England sea-coast.

Lucy in middle years.

In 1875, Fields hired Lucy to edit a new children's magazine called *Our Young Folks*. It was enormously popular and went on, in the form of its successor, *St. Nicholas*, well into the twentieth century, when it was read by Edna St. Vincent Millay and Jack London, who were inspired to send their juvenile pieces to the magazine.

The most famous piece of fiction in *Our Young Folks* was "The Story of a Bad Boy," by Thomas Bailey Aldrich. The "bad" boy hero was the first breaking away from the ideal heroes and heroines of children's literature. These characters were not so much bad, as human and natural pranksters. The tradition was carried on by Wilbur Peck in *Peck's Bad Boy* and Mark Twain in his Tom Sawyer and Huckleberry Finn stories.

The magazine published the work of Harriet Beecher Stowe, Louisa May Alcott, Henry Wadsworth Longfellow—and John Greenleaf Whittier. Whittier sent Lucy a poem called "In School-Days." Accompanying it was a note. "Be honest with it," he said, "and if it seems too spooney for a grave Quaker like myself, don't compromise me by printing it."

Lucy loved the poem as did everyone who read it. It was a humorous and touching tale of an elderly man who recalls that when he was very young a girl said to him:

"I'm sorry that I spelt the word:
I hate to go above you,
Because,"—the brown eyes lower fell—
Because you see, I love you!"

This was very "spooney" for a man who attracted women by the score, but would never let a single one get romantically involved with him.

Lucy herself wrote poems for the magazine, many of which were later collected in a book called *Childhood Songs*, but her main contribution was her editorial commentary in a column called "Our Letter Box." The magazine had about fifty thousand subscribers and received about a thousand letters a month. Lucy read them all and published the most interesting ones. To the readers who asked questions or wanted advice, she provided answers. One child wanted to know if her desire to be a writer when she was grown was a wise one. Lucy answered:

A writer's life is not so easy as it seems. If you undertake it, you must be prepared to meet discouragement which nothing but an intense love of your work will overcome. Write, if you cannot help it—but do not depend upon writing "for a living" if you can find anything else to do.

Some of the poetry in the magazine became part of an anthology called *Child Life,* edited by Whittier and Lucy together. Lucy was the only one Whittier ever collaborated with on any project. This was followed by *Child Life in Prose.* While collecting the material to go into the book, Lucy became ill, but continued working so as to meet the publisher's deadline. Spurring her on, Whittier wrote, "It will be a good time while thee are shut indoors to turn to that dreadful book, which should have the benefit of thy reflection, whether sick or well, as the ancient Germans debated all matters twice, once drunk, and once sober."

Although she did more than her share of the work on both books and a third one they edited together, Lucy's name did not appear on any of the title pages. Whittier sent her part of his royalty payments and that was all. What Lucy thought of that arrangement was not recorded. She worshipped Whittier and was grateful for his friendship and inspiration.

In 1891, when Lucy was sixty-seven and Whittier eighty-four, Lucy asked his permission to dedicate a book to him. She said in a note, using his Quaker form of address: *I shall never forget how beautiful the world has been to me, through thee.*

Lucy was by then herself a widely-read poet with an adoring readership. Numerous writers found her work praiseworthy. Harriet Beecher Stowe called her the American Elizabeth Barrett Browning. Henry Wadsworth Longfellow wrote her a complimentary note. Oliver Wendell Holmes wrote touching lines about his reactions to her work:

> My Dear Miss Larcom,
> I have been reading your poems at all the spare moments that I could find this evening. My wife and daughter were sitting opposite me, and I had to shade my eyes with my hand that they should not see the tears shining in them.

However, it was not her poetry, but a work of prose that Lucy tossed off in 1889 with apparently little effort, that would be her true gift to future readers. It was a slender volume called A New England Girlhood.

It was written, she said, "for girls of all ages, and women who have not forgotten their girlhood," in the hope that they would take life as it came to them and "live it faithfully, looking and striving always toward better life."

A New England Girlhood is a winning account of the flowering of a creative artist from most simple elements of life. Lucy had no important forbears, but prided herself on her "inheritance of hard work." The town of Beverly was an ordinary seaside community, made colorful by the foreign trade of its seafaring men. Women wore shawls from China and silks and satins from Turkey. Children played with Russian kopeks and British halfpennies, and admired the faces of visitors from other countries, with their handsome darker skins and striking Asian features.

There were no obviously rich or poor people in the Beverly of the 1830s. Everyone seemed to work with his or her hands. And so the transition to work in the mills seemed like a natural one. But instead of life in a drowsy village, with each family shut in behind closed doors, Lucy now had the stimulation of a city, where each one's affairs were important to the other. Her pulse quickened and her senses became alert. Her exposure to the printed word brought out her latent talent. But it was the discipline of work that perhaps taught her more than anything else. She learned that only through hard effort could one achieve, and that individuals are part of a universal network.

This we working-girls might have learned from the webs of cloth we saw woven around us. Every little thread must take its place as warp or woof, and keep in it steadily.

A *New England Girlhood* received a more personal response from its readers than any of her other books. Letters arrived almost every day after the book was published.

Unlike Sarah Bagley and Harriet Hanson Robinson, Lucy could not "club" herself, as she put it. Although she had strong abolitionist sentiments, she had never become part of an antislavery group. She felt that to go out on strike was "unwomanly." When most of her friends were working for woman suffrage, she observed the movement as an outsider, writing to her old friend Harriet in 1870 that she was "on the fence" on such matters.

If she was indeed a woman of the century, it was in the example she set: a "mill girl poet" who began as a child laborer and, against all odds, rose to recognition in the literary world. She left behind her fifteen volumes of her own work, most of them poetry, and again as many books of collections of others' work which she edited. She was one of the rare artists who was able in her own lifetime to know that she had been a success.

George Edward Woodberry, a literary critic and professor, born in the same town as Lucy Larcom, delivered a memorial address after her death in 1893. "It was a life well lived," he concluded in his eloquent piece:

And yet, the significant thing in it is not that she caught the beauty of these fields and woods, and the sea that we look on by day and night, not that she praised the lowly life and illustrated them in herself with simplicity and power, not that she used the flowers of our wayside for parables . . . but rather that she showed in the total unity of her life and work, that the pursuit of an ideal, is the surest pledge that a life shall be nobly led itself, and have the greatest utility to others.

And Woodberry ended with her own line: *Climb for the white flower of your dream!*

BOOK TWO

Harriet Hanson
Robinson
1825 - 1911

1

And a Little Child Shall Lead Them

NINE-year-old Harriet sits in the backyard of her mother's company-owned boardinghouse, scouring silverware. It is a Saturday, a cold and damp morning in February, 1834. Voices can be heard from a distant street. After a time the sound is more like a roar.

"What could that be?" Mrs. Hanson asks, looking out the back door.

"Why don't I run down the street and see?" Harriet runs off, disregarding her mother's troubled expression.

It is surprising to see so many operatives on the streets at eleven in the morning when they normally worked until three on Saturdays. They are coming out of the various mills in small and large groups. Some of the girls are waving handkerchiefs at the faces looking out of the mill windows.

Someone tells Harriet that this is a turnout in protest of a fifteen percent wage cut. She follows the people to the public square of Lowell where a speakers' platform is being hastily erected.

The crowd has grown to almost a thousand, spilling over into several streets. A young woman with a bonnet tied firmly under her chin addresses the crowd, little puffs of air becoming visible when she pauses for a breath. Harriet has never seen a woman speak in public and feels embarrassed for the speaker, who herself shows no signs of hesitation. Her voice rings out like a trumpet. She talks about the "monied aristocracy" and how they lord it over the "daughters

Merrimack Street in Lowell.

of freemen" who work for them. She reads from a long petition which ends with the poem:

> Let oppression shrug her shoulders,
> And a haughty tyrant frown,
> And little upstart Ignorance,
> In mockery look down,
> Yet I value not the feeble threats
> Of tories in disguise
> While the flag of Independence
> O'er our noble nation flies.

This turnout lasts only a few days but the girls create a near financial panic when they withdraw all

---

their savings from the bank. Many simply go home, getting all the wagons and carts they can find to carry their belongings. The owners of the mills are glad to see so many depart. The agent of the Lawrence Corporation writes to his treasurer: "This afternoon we have paid off several of these Amazons & presume they will leave town on Monday."

All of this made a strong impression on Harriet, and, in 1836, when she was eleven and working as a doffer in the mills, she took part in a similar occurrence. This time the wage cut had come in the form of a levy on the girls' wages to increase the amount given to the boardinghouse matrons.

The turnout was many days in preparation. Harriet had listened to all the discussions and was more than ready to leave the Spinning Room when the signal was given. The other girls in her room were shy or undecided and stood there neither working nor moving. "Well," Harriet said loudly, "I don't care who turns out. *I* am going now." The other girls followed her into the street. This time thousands marched in a procession, one quarter of the entire working population. One of the mills was said to be in a "state of rebellion" and the mood was contagious.

The marchers sang a parody to a popular song with the title "I Won't be a Nun:"

> *Oh, isn't it a pity*
> *Such a pretty girl as I*

Should be sent to the factory
To pine away and die?
Oh, I cannot be a slave,
I will not be a slave,
For I'm so fond of liberty
That I cannot be a slave.

Shortly afterward, a temporary Factory Girls' Association was formed, numbering twenty-five hundred. Greetings came from a workingmen's group, the National Trades Union, which was convening at the time in another state. They promised to do all within their power to help the brave women who were "standing out against the oppression of the soulless employers." In spite of all the support, the turnout petered out, but this time it had lasted almost a month, and some of the mills reversed the wage cut.

Harriet's family was to suffer in a way she had not foreseen. Her mother, who had been several years widowed, depended for an income on her position as boardinghouse matron. According to the story told by Harriet many years later, the agent paid her a call and said, "Mrs. Hanson, you could not prevent the older girls among your boarders from turning out, but your daughter is a child, and *her* you could control." And with that he told the woman that she was relieved of her job. Although she would find another boardinghouse to run, this was a great hardship on the family.

However wearying it was for the little doffers

to be locked in the mills thirteen hours a day, they knew they were more fortunate than their English counterparts. They read Elizabeth Barrett Browning's poem, "Cry of the Children," with its heartrending line: *Oh ye wheels, stop, be silent for today!*

British children, recruited from the poorhouses, sometimes along with their mothers, would start to work as young as five years of age. If they got drowsy at their tasks they could be whipped or slapped. It was not unusual for an overseer to dump a bucket of water over the head of a child weaver whose head was nodding. It was said that rooming house beds never grew cold, for when the night shift scrambled out of them, the day shift crawled in. These mill children looked as old and tired as adults by the time they reached their teens.

In the United States, child labor would not be a problem until later in the nineteenth century, when one quarter of the workers in the southern mills were under sixteen. In Lowell, so long as there were young women in what seemed to be a never-ending stream, there was no need for youngsters to do the difficult tasks.

The 1837 law requiring three months of schooling for mill children was one of the first pieces of labor legislation in Massachusetts.

Harriet went to the North Grammar School at the same time as Lucy Larcom did. It was at the bot-

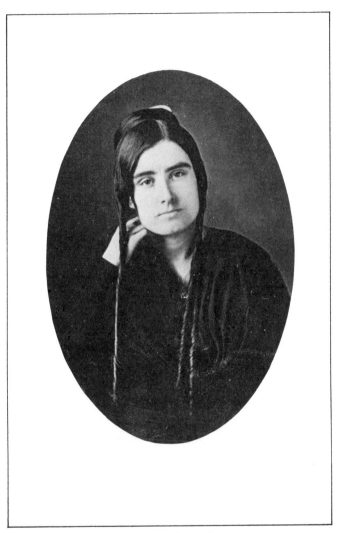

Harriet at 18 in 1843.

tom of a hill on which the children coasted in the winter and played in the summer. There was a cave under the hill where they acted out scenes from their favorite stories. Harriet suffered with the same Master Hill as Lucy did, and blossomed under the benign administration. But, unlike Lucy, Harriet was able to go on to high school. This was because her brother John, later to be a minister, was helping out by working as a clerk at the counting house of the Tremont mill.

The first high school was over a butcher shop, but soon it moved into a building of its own. It was the first public high school for both boys and girls, and its prospectus said that

> *its object is to place within reach of the poorest citizen such means of preparing his children for college, or for giving instruction for any branch of active business, as the richest.*

Harriet got excellent grades at school, particularly in composition. She wrote pieces with such weighty titles as "Poverty is not Disgraceful" and "Indolence and Industry."

Her brother John, who was only two years older, held up high standards for her. Once, when Harriet said "I done it," John looked her in the eye, a hand on her shoulder, and said firmly: "You *done* it! Don't let

A drawing-in girl preparing the warp threads for the loom. This was Harriet's favorite work in the mill.

me hear you say *I done it* again, unless you can use *have* or *had* before it."

The agent of the Tremont mill kept lost or confiscated books in his desk. He allowed John to take them home overnight or on weekends. Most of them were books of poetry. Harriet memorized as many poems as she could. She boasted that she knew all the work of Henry Wadsworth Longfellow, and the poems stayed with her for life.

Since breakfast in the boardinghouses was often taken before daylight, Mrs. Hanson prepared it the night before. As Harriet helped her heat it the next morning, she would hold a book in one hand. One of the boarders had a membership in Lowell's rental library and Harriet arranged to read all the books she borrowed by offering to carry them to and from the library. In this way she got to read the major novelists of the day like Scott, Fielding and Smollett. The library was so heavily used that the owner of a circulating library in Dover, New Hampshire, another mill town, moved to Lowell with his stock of two thousand volumes.

Inevitably all this reading inspired Harriet to write. After two years in high school Harriet became a drawing-in girl. Drawing-in was one of the few hand processes in the mill and only about a dozen girls worked at it. They sat in the dressing room, where the warp threads were starched and drew those threads one by one into a harness, making them ready for the loom. Harriet, like Lucy Larcom, chose lower-paid work, and for the same reasons. Since the work was unpressured they could steal time to think and write. Harriet kept a large blank book into which she recorded bits of verse, ideas and quotations from her reading. Harriet did not have to observe the ten o'clock curfew, since her mother was in charge of the boardinghouse and so could put pen to paper far into the night.

"Beautiful thoughts are like dewdrops," she wrote in one piece. "They come not from heaven, but from the plants which they nourish." She wrote a poem on the death of the poet Percy Bysshe Shelley, beginning, "I call to the earth to lament—Shelley is dead."

Death also was a common theme among these healthy young women. It was a process Lucy Larcom referred to as "dismalizing." But one of Harriet's poems on the subject was based on a real family tragedy. One day in November, 1836, Harriet's brother "little Willie" Hanson, aged seven, had wandered away from the boardinghouse while his mother was busy with her numerous chores. Playing along the Merrimack River, the child had accidentally fallen in and was drowned. By the time they had discovered he was missing, the boy's body had been washed ashore at Plum Island, forty miles down the river. Willie had been buried on the Island in a nameless grave, since the family could not afford a formal burial. Ten years after that tragic event, Harriet wrote her poem about Willie, "the brightest and best" of them all. She called it "The Dying Boy" and brought it to the offices of the

I can't forget! I can't forget!
The lovely, gentle Harriet,
Whose first glance filled my soul with love;
As pure as Seraphs know above

I can't forget! I can't forget!
Her lovely form and eyes of jet,
Those eyes which caused me first to feel
The pangs which she alone can heal.

I can't forget! I can't forget!
That oft our thought of Harriet
Has chased my sorrow far away,
And turned my midnight into day.

Do not forget! Do not forget!
That I most truly love you yet,
But one kind smile on me bestow,
To light me thro' this world of woe,

      Ever thine
      My Valentine.

Lowell Courier, which had published the mill girls' writings from time to time.

The assistant editor of the newspaper, William Stevens Robinson, was interested in the poem, but even more in the young woman poet. Harriet was then just over twenty. She had a face of extraordinary beauty, with pale skin and long dark hair.

Robinson was six years older than Harriet, a man of medium height with a self-effacing manner that made one overlook him in any group. But his wit slipped out sometimes when he was speaking. It would make him one of the most trenchant journalists of his day.

A romance was on. On Saint Valentine's Day of 1847, Harriet received a passionate and sentimental Valentine from William. Part of it read:

> *I can't forget! I can't forget!*
> *Her lovely form and eyes of jet,*
> *Those eyes that caused me first to feel*
> *The pangs which she alone can heal.*
>
> *I can't forget! I can't forget!*
> *That oft one thought of Harriet*
> *Has chased my sorrows far away,*
> *And turned my midnight into day.*

A Valentine from William to Harriet, written during their courtship.

2

Bride in Bronze Shoes

IT WAS not surprising that the improvement circles should attract Harriet. What was, perhaps, surprising was that she attended so few. Had she known that she would be the historian of this early effort at self-improvement and of the magazine that resulted from it, she might have been more attentive.

Since the *Offering* had been published by the same William Schouler who was the owner of the *Courier*, her beau William Robinson was just a few doors from where the circle met most of the time. The two editors, Harriet Farley and Harriot Curtis, got on well together. Farley was ambitious and genteel. She liked to write the editorials and had a way with the "editorial 'we'." Curtis had a sharp and startling way of speaking and writing, but was contented in most matters to take a back seat.

On a day Harriet Hanson attended the circle, part of a novel of Curtis's was read. She had already had a novel published and seemed to have a brilliant career before her. A prose poem of Lucy Larcom's was also read. It seemed a marvel to Harriet that someone so young could have such a mature talent. Another poem was read, which described the wind as taking "the tall trees by the hair, and as with besoms swept the air." Harriet could not understand why comparing trees to heads caused such mirth. Likely as not it was the use of the word "besoms," meaning brooms, and its similarity to the word "bosoms." Several of Harriet's poems did appear in the *Offering*, but she was a minor contributor.

Lowell had become a great curiosity on the continent. Factory girls who organized and sat through classes, who packed the lecture halls and who published whole magazines—what a phenomenon! It was the corporations who were generally complimented for their good-natured benevolence, when it should have been the women themselves for wanting learning and culture so badly that they devoted every precious minute and their scant energies to getting it.

Beginning in the 1830s, all travelers wanting to see typical American sights, stopped at Lowell. Foreigners always tried to visit at least one school, one prison, one Native American community, an insane asylum, a Southern plantation—and Lowell.

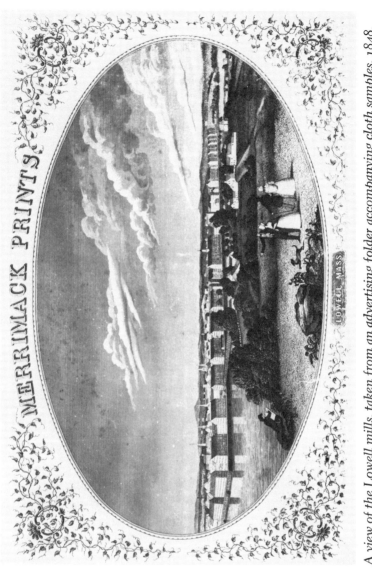

A view of the Lowell mills, taken from an advertising folder accompanying cloth samples, 1848.

Michel Chevalier, sent by the French government to study American transportation and public works, found the city as fresh as an opera setting. It looked to him like a doll's world made of pasteboard: the new brick factories, the "very neat, very snug" boardinghouses, the "fancy goods" shops, banks, schools and churches. He compared the mills to Spanish convents, but the new nuns "instead of working sacred hearts, spin and weave cotton."

Davy Crockett, "King of the Wild Frontier," was given a suit made of American broadcloth by the owners of the mills. This stirred in him enormous fervor when he described his trip in a book which would sell extremely well, *An Account of Colonel Crockett's Tour to the North and Down East.* He talked about the miracle of turning Southern cotton into cheap cloth and then described a visit to the mills:

> *We stopped at a large stone house at the head of the falls of the Merrimack River, and having taken a little refreshment, went down among the factories. The dinner bells were ringing and the folks pouring out of the houses like bees out of gum. I looked at them as they passed, all well-dressed, lively and genteel in their appearance, indeed the girls looked as if they were coming from a quilting frolic.*

In June, 1933, Andrew Jackson, the president of the United States, came to view this industrial wonderland. Standing on the balcony of the largest hotel in the city, Jackson viewed the procession of local militia, some mounted infantry from Lowell and neighboring towns, followed by five hundred children on a school holiday carrying flowers. But the high point of the day was the parade of two thousand mill girls, ranked by corporation. Each wore a lovely white muslin dress with a blue sash and carried a green or blue parasol. They were all to have been green, but there were not enough to be found in all the shops of Boston and New York. The president bowed his head to each group that passed and was heard to say, "Very pretty women, by God!"

The visitors who came later found an "idyl" that was somewhat tarnished. And they looked at the situation with greater depth. By the mid-1840s turnouts, petitions and labor conventions had shown that dissatisfaction was spreading among the workers, who were doing more for less money than they had a decade earlier.

Catherine Beecher, an educator, and the sister of Harriet Beecher Stowe (author of *Uncle Tom's Cabin*) was on a tour of the country in 1845, investigating the lives of women and children. She spoke not only to the operatives, but to agents, overseers, ministers and doctors. She spent hours in the mills, watching the pounding of the shuttles through the looms and the whirling of the spindles, breathing the dense air, and racing to hastily-eaten meals.

Had some local physician claimed that there were fewer deaths in Lowell? Of course there were fewer deaths, she said. Almost the entire working population consisted of young people. And if any of them were gravely ill, they went back to their rural homes to be nursed to health, or to die. Told about the lectures and classes so popular among the women, Beecher said that in her opinion they should have stayed in bed! "Every moment devoted to lectures, study, or writing," she wrote, "must be a robbery on health, and worse than nothing."

Whittier in his brief stay in Lowell at about the same time, had mixed feelings about what he observed. On the one hand he saw women and men on an equal footing. He was impressed that the same hands that tended a power loom could also write essays and poetry. But he was frightened by this new Gospel of Work preached from the enormous brick cathedrals. He saw the operatives setting out to work before dawn and returning weary to their rooms after a brutal thirteen-hour day. In late September began the "lighting up," as hundreds of oil lamps were lit to keep the workers toiling after sunset. From a distance, Whittier watched the figures of the operatives silhouetted in the many windows of the mills, doing their work dance. It was fascinating to the eye, but depressing to the soul. "Every web which falls from these restless looms," Whittier wrote in the newspaper he was editing, "has a history more or less connected with sin and suffering, beginning with slavery and ending with overwork and premature death."

Sixty years after she began working in Lowell as a doffer, Harriet would write the book *Loom and Spindle; Or, Life Among the Early Mill Girls*. Like Lucy Larcom's *A New England Girlhood*, it was a personal account of a unique time in labor history, and it shared with that book a major weakness. It saw Lowell through the mists of time, with many of the rough edges rubbed smooth. Both Robinson and Larcom were attempting to create the image of an aristocracy of labor, when the Yankee working girl was queen for a day. As part of the picture it was invaluable.

Harriet caught the distinct personality types who populated the mills. There was the middle-aged maiden aunt of the New England household, referred to in wills as "relicts" and "incumbrances," who had been completely dependent on the working men of her extended family. They came to Lowell "depressed, modest, mincing, hardly daring to look one in the face." Within a short time they were transformed:

After the first pay-day came, and they felt the jingle of silver in their pockets, their bowed heads were lifted, their necks seemed braced with steel, they looked you in the face, sang blithely among their looms and frames, and walked with elastic step to and from work. How sedately gay in their new attire they walked to church, and how proudly they dropped their silver fourpence into the contribution-box!

Label appearing on finished cloth.

There was the runaway wife, who would hide behind the looms whenever the mill had visitors, afraid of a husband who might force her to return to bed and board, or more typically, "trustee" the wife's wage, for a husband could legally claim his estranged wife's earnings. Many such women used false names.

She showed the new urban female, who, although a lowly operative, could dress in the latest Boston fashions. Middle class women were offended by this, for it was difficult to tell who was a "lady" and who was not. "How stands the difference now?" asked the editor of the stylish *Godey's Lady's Book*. "Many of the factory girls wear gold watches, and an imitation, at least, of all the ornaments which grace the daughters of our most opulent citizens!"

Harriet told an amusing story of a working girl who became the wife of an overseer. She suddenly assumed such airs that one of her old acquaintances in the mill referred to the street where the overseers lived as "Puckersville." Once, when visiting the weave room of her old mill, she pointed up at belts and pulleys and asked with apparent innocence, "What's them things up there?"

Harriet herself left work to marry in 1848, although she certainly did not enter the leisure class in so doing. On Thanksgiving Day Harriet and William said their vows in a small ceremony in William's brother's house in Salem.

The twenty-three-year-old bride wore a long white dress with a white satin sash and laced bronze shoes. All she remembered of that evening was the pattern of the carpet under her feet.

William wrote to his mother, who was unable to attend:

> *Hatty will help take care of me now, mother—you have done it all along & I hope I shall never be ungrateful for your goodness in bringing me up till thirty years old—and bringing me up well, I think.*

Before six months had passed, William would be unemployed! His habit of speaking "God's truth" would invariably put him at odds with editors of newspapers, and he would be dropped like a hot coal. One solution was to start a paper of his own. He did so, but even this venture would fail before too long.

3

A Stab in the Dark

IN THE small hours of the morning on a wintry night in 1850, a midwife shook the sleeping William by the shoulder and announced, "It's a girl!"

"*What's* a girl?" the drowsy man asked, and then he remembered. His wife had been about to give birth.

Harriette Lucy, the first of the Robinsons' children, was brought "gently and deliberately" into life, as the proud mother recorded in her diary. And those words exactly describe how Hattie, as this daughter would be called, would conduct herself in life.

Two more children followed, each two years apart: Elizabeth Osborne, named after a Lowell friend of Harriet's who had died young, and William Elbridge. This "Willie" did not live even as long as his namesake, Harriet's brother who had drowned in the Merrimack. Five years later Edward Warrington, the fourth and last child, was born. He was nicknamed "Warrie."

While the children were small, William was trying to make a success of a new antislavery newspaper
called the *Lowell American*. The year Hattie was born
was an important year in the struggle against "the peculiar institution," as slavery was called. The Fugitive
Slave Act was passed by Congress. It stated that the
owner of an escaped slave needed no proof to identify
his former slave, and no matter what state the former

The Robinson children: Lizzie, Warrie and Hattie.

slave had escaped to, the owner could demand his or her return. The black person so named could neither say nor do anything on his own behalf, and if anyone tried to help him or her, the individual would be subject to up to a one thousand dollar fine and six months in jail.

This false "justice" turned many New Englanders from merely passive observers of slavery into active abolitionists. They watched as blacks were mistakenly identified or misidentified and virtually kidnapped into servitude.

A famous case tried under this act in Massachusetts was the Anthony Burns case. Burns's lawyer was Richard Henry Dana, who had written the popular novel *Two Years Before the Mast*. A vigilance committee was formed to guarantee that Burns not be returned to his Virginia "master."

Crowds filled Faneuil Hall in Boston to capacity that evening in May, 1854, when Wendell Phillips, the famous abolitionist preacher, urged them to "see to it that Anthony Burns has no master but his God!" An attempt was made to break into the courthouse where Burns was kept and to free him. Instead a virtual army of eleven thousand soldiers escorted Burns to the boat taking him back to Virginia.

As a result of a rousing article by Robinson, Judge Loring, who had tried the Burns case, was later removed "for disobedience to the Personal Liberty law, in permitting this kidnapping of Anthony Burns."

The Whig Party, more liberal than the Democratic Party of the time, was divided into "Cotton" and "Conscience" Whigs. The Cotton Whigs endorsed the slave system, which supplied the thriving textile industry with its raw materials, while the Conscience Whigs could not abide the brutal subjugation of one human being by another for whatever reason. Robinson's position was even more militant.

While Robinson was working for the *Courier*, he had refused to support the popular candidate for President, old "rough and ready" Zachary Taylor, who had made a reputation for himself in the Mexican-American War. His owning slaves was only one of the reasons Robinson withheld his allegiance. One day two agents from the Lowell corporations called on him and told him they would see to it that he kept his job if he changed his position. He refused to do this and eventually had to leave the newspaper. John Greenleaf Whittier sent his approval of Robinson's stand: "I heartily congratulate thee," he wrote, "on thy emancipation from the Taylor party."

Robinson then founded the *American* and kept it going for almost five years, but it was a difficult time for the family. Harriet had to manage on an income of four hundred dollars a year. Old clothing was continually resewn and remodeled. When part of the rug wore out, it was cut and patched together again. She

William Stevens Robinson.

could not have managed all the housework, if not for the help of her mother, who had come to live with them. Almost every week friends sent gifts of money and food. Robinson was so short-staffed at the paper that he often set the type himself, writing the articles as he went along!

The Robinsons loved reading aloud from books in the evening. They had an almost endless supply from the review copies that were sent to the newspaper. Robinson's happiest moments were spent sitting at a table in his parlor scribbling his articles while his children played around him and his wife sewed or knitted. Every few hours he would laugh aloud at his own humor, startling the family.

Like most women then, Harriet was contented with living in the shadow of her husband's career. But sometimes she resented not being part of all the political activity going on around her. Once a few of Robinson's abolitionist friends came to call, all men. They talked about the events of the day: the indifference of the Whig Party to the slavery issue, how fugitive slaves were forced to return to their inhuman bosses, and so on. Harriet sat listening raptly, while rocking a cradle. Finally the gentlemen rose to leave. They were almost out the door, when one of them turned and spoke to Harriet for the first time. "Dreadful weather we're having, don't you think so, Mrs. Robinson?" What she answered is not recorded, but she did make note of the incident later on.

The women working in the textile mills were aware that they were spinning and weaving cotton grown by Southern slaves. Lucy Larcom wrote about those feelings years afterward in *An Idyl of Work*:

> When I've thought what soil the cotton-plant
> We weave is rooted in, what waters it—
> The blood of souls in bondage—I have felt
> That I was sinning against the light to stay
> And turn the accursed fibre into cloth.

97

While the "lords of the loom and the lords of the lash" cooperated, the mill girls signed many petitions against slavery to ease their consciences.

When Lincoln was elected President, Robinson, now with the majority party, was offered any job that he wished connected with the Massachusetts legislature. But always more principled than practical, he refused to take an office to which he was not elected. Finally, in 1862, when the Civil War was raging, he was legally elected clerk of the state's House of Representatives, a job he was to hold for ten years.

In the last years of his clerkship, Robinson gathered material for a book that would be the definitive manual on parliamentary procedure. In 1870, twenty-year-old Hattie began to help him in his office in the state house, and in 1872, she was officially appointed his assistant. This made her the first woman to be an official in any legislature in the country. To cope with any stares from the male legislators, she kept very busy taking notes. Several bills in favor of woman suffrage were placed on the House agenda by Robinson, working with a sympathetic legislator.

All this time Robinson was building a reputation for himself, writing articles for various newspapers under the pen name of "Warrington." He had admirers all over the country. A friend of the family's visiting in Kansas saw someone absorbed in one of the Warrington pieces. "I always read the *Springfield*

Republican," the man told him, "just to see what that
fellow Warrington has to say. I can't get along without reading it." These "Warrington letters" were a
free vehicle for Robinson to air all his opinions on
politics, to write word portraits of men he considered
important, and to champion what appeared to be lost
causes.

To those people he wanted to criticize he could
be "potent and piercing." In doing so he made a powerful enemy of Benjamin Franklin Butler. Like Robinson, Butler was a self-made man, but in contrast to
Robinson, he had few scruples, changing parties and
allegiances when it suited him.

In his younger, idealistic years, Butler had sup-
ported the struggle for a ten-hour work day. In the
days before the secret ballot, a notice had been put up
on the gate of one of the Lowell mills: *Whoever, employed by this corporation, votes the Butler ten-hour
ticket on Monday night, will be discharged.*

Later, as a lawyer, when Butler defended an
obvious scoundrel, Robinson had called him to task
publicly. His response was to walk into Robinson's
office, knock his eyeglasses off, and walk out. Eventually Butler became governor of the state and even
ran for president. He never forgot his ardent critic.

On hearing that Butler would see to it that he
was voted out of his clerkship, Robinson said, "If Butler's gang can defeat me, let them do so." He was

confident of keeping his office, but in 1873, his opponent got the better of him, and he was voted out. Again Robinson was approached to sell out, and promised his job back if he did, and again he would not compromise his principles. Harriet called his defeat "a stab in the dark." Even his friends in the legislature became cool to him, once he had been dropped.

A broken man, Robinson lost his health and never regained it. He died at the age of fifty-eight, saying to Harriet, "I am going to leave you to make the struggle all over again." Harriet recorded those words in her diary and added later on: ". . . and I have made it."

4

Frowns and Stares

IT IS 1880. There is an election in Malden, Massachusetts, where the Robinson family has been settled for many years. The previous year the Massachusetts legislature had passed a law permitting women to vote for their towns' school committees. But it would be another forty years until women could vote for president, congressmen and state legislators.

Harriet and Hattie have helped to round up the fifty women in Malden who will vote. Hattie was the first woman in Massachusetts to register to vote for any official—another first for her.

The two dress carefully, knowing they will be on display as they promenade from their home to Malden's Town Hall. Harriet's mother, Mrs. Hanson, somewhat feeble at eighty-five, has decided to stay home, even though she has registered.

As they walk, people stare at them. Shopkeepers leave their shops to see the strange phenomenon of women daring to vote. Their grocer tells them a "male uprising" is awaiting them at the town hall.

There is no uprising, but a group of idle men begin to heckle them as they walk in to vote. One of them points to his crony and says loudly: "Is *them* some 'iv 'em?"

When Hattie had been assistant clerk she had sat in on a hearing of the Judicial Committee on Woman Suffrage. Lucy Stone, a short woman with a silvery voice, had handled every male supremacist argument raised by the legislators with extraordinary aplomb. Hattie reported this to Harriet and the two decided they would catch the next public appearance of Lucy Stone. They did so, heard a long speech, "full of law, logic and illustrations" and were sold on the suffrage struggle.

"The woman's hour has struck!" Robinson had written, shortly before his death. This was true in more ways than one. Women were getting involved in many of the social struggles of their day: racism, labor issues, temperance, the double standard in morality, concern about the poor, compassion for the treatment of prisoners and inmates of other institutions. Many of the organizations they formed were exclusively female.

Women were also writing. In midcentury there were more women writing fiction than men. They created a whole genre, the domestic novel, and contributed poetry and prose to newspapers, magazines and gift annuals.

Harriet herself had published a collection of "Warrington's" writings at her own expense, writing an introduction almost as long as the book. Going on the road to peddle the book and raise money, she made good her expenses and more. Hattie was writing stories for children. Eventually she would have six books published.

When Harriet and Hattie joined the suffrage movement, it was splitting into two factions. The two groups had almost the same names: one called itself the American Woman Suffrage Association, the other the National Woman Suffrage Association. The "Nationals," led by Susan B. Anthony and Elizabeth Cady Stanton, had a more aggressive program. They felt that getting the right to vote was only half the battle for women. They were concerned about women's rights at home and in the workplace. Their publication, *The Revolution*, reported on early women's clubs, activity among female laundry workers, type-setters and tailors, as well as on feminist activity abroad. The "Americans," led by Lucy Stone and her husband, Henry Blackwell, felt that giving attention to the one issue of the vote would be more effective.

Eventually the two groups were to merge, but for twenty years they conducted activities in parallel. Harriet and Hattie worked with the Nationals. Harriet was particularly good at planning fund-raising fairs and bazaars. Hattie was an excellent speaker, feminine and demure, good at winning over male audiences.

After the Malden vote, Harriet composed a poem that appeared in one of the fair booklets:

What's the news of the day,
Good neighbor, I pray?
Oh! women are trying to vote, they say;
The men who were there,
with frown and with stare,
Looked on with amazement that women should dare;
And one old man sighed,
And wished he had died,
Ere he saw such a day of sorrow and care.
Let the old fogies rave,
We still will be brave,
And our rights to the ballot persistently crave;
When woman is free
Only then there can be
In our happy country no longer a slave.

In the 1870s some brave women voted illegally when they had a chance to, in order to attract attention to their cause. In the election of 1872, Susan B. Anthony and fifteen others defied authority in

Rochester, New York, and registered and then voted. Anthony was charged with "knowingly, wrongfully and unlawfully voting for a representative to the Congress of the United States." She was not allowed to testify in court, but was found guilty and fined one hundred dollars. Before the sentence was served the judge asked her if she had anything to say, a tactical error on his part. Anthony delivered a talk that blistered the ears of the judge and the jury.

One of the strategies of the movement was to get individual states to pass suffrage laws. The ones most responsive were the newly settled frontier states. Hattie was such an eloquent speaker that she was sent to "stump" Nebraska in 1882 and had four or five speeches to deliver each week she was there. She was shocked to find herself the butt of ridicule on anti-suffrage posters. The *Omaha Herald* reported that "the suffering sisters are howling over woman's rights on the stump," and referred to Hattie as part of a "shrieking sisterhood."

Back home at Malden, the woman's rights people were treated with sexist amusement. When a leading suffrage speaker came to town, a minister announced to his congregation: "This evening at Town Hall a hen will attempt to crow!" When a group of the women met to plan strategies, the meeting was referred to in the press as a "Hen Convention." Sometimes it seemed as if women were "so many zeroes or nothings in the sum of humanity," Harriet said in one of her many eloquent speeches.

In 1882, Harriet, as one of the movement's leading workers, was the first woman to testify before a congressional committee on the subject of suffrage. She watched the senators' faces change from boredom and indifference to "interest mingled with surprise," as her speech progressed.

Harriet's book, *Massachusetts in the Woman Suffrage Movement*, published in 1881, in 1886 became a chapter in the six-volume work, *History of Woman Suffrage*, edited by Stanton, Anthony and others.

It took seven decades of struggle for women to win the vote. Hattie would be seventy, as old as the movement itself, when finally, in 1920, the nineteenth, or "Anthony Amendment" to the Constitution was passed, and women could vote for the president of their country.

In 1895, when a child was born to her son Warrie, Harriet was gratified that she was named Harriet Hanson Robinson II, and that she was "born to freedom" in Colorado, a state that had passed a woman suffrage law.

5

The New Pandora

IT IS January 26, 1888, and Harriet's play, "Captain Mary Miller," is being performed at Union Hall in Boston. The previous year it had been published as a book. Tickets at thirty-five and fifty cents each are sold out. Hattie is making her stage debut playing the heroine's mother, complete with a salty midwestern drawl.

The message is a feminist one. It is the true story of a Captain Mary Miller, who took over a river boat on the Mississippi when her husband got too sick to run it. The owner of the boat is outraged that a woman has the nerve to want to be Captain:

> Mr. Romberg: *I don't see how you can run this boat.*
>
> Mary (rising): *Why not, sir? I have run her for the last three or four months. I carried*

her way up the Red and Yellow, and down
again to Baton Rouge, through the most
crooked part of the whole thousand-mile
route; and I steered her most of the time
myself. The mate don't know much about
handling the wheel.

Mr. Romberg: *You may run the boat but you*
cannot as Captain—you have no license. . . .

Mary somehow manages to get the license, and when
her husband is well again, it is she, not he who re-
mains the Captain.

A year later Harriet published a book-length
poem, rewriting the Greek myth of Pandora. In the
original story, Pandora, which meant "all gifts," was
sent to earth by the God Zeus, to punish all mortal
men. She was given a mysterious box and when curiosity overwhelmed her and she opened it, all the sor-
rows and evils of the world were released. As she
snapped the box shut, only hope remained inside.

In Harriet's version Pandora, representing
woman, brings not sorrow, but beauty, civilization
and hope to the world. Pandora says:

That I am a woman doth not define my scope.
Sex cannot limit the immortal mind.
We are ourselves, with individual souls,
Still struggling onward toward the infinite.

The Woman's Journal, the magazine of the "American" wing of the suffrage movement had nothing but praise for the book. They compared some of the lines to Shakespeare's. Lucy Larcom, writing a review for the *Portland Transcript,* spoke of the poetry as a "strong chant, as classical in its strain as some of Shelley's in his imaginative dramas."

The idea for *Loom and Spindle* came from Susan B. Anthony, who thought that it would be a splendid idea if someone would write something about Lowell's mill girl magazine. Harriet took up the challenge and wrote her charming memoir, printing it at her own expense. These short sketches of *Offering* contributors were supposed to have been accompanied by photographs or portraits, but funds ran out. Reprinted in 1976, *Loom and Spindle* insures Harriet Hanson Robinson a secure place in the pantheon of historians of women's history.

Harriet and Hattie made an additional contribution to the welfare of the women of their time. In the 1870s, middle class women, excluded from most organizations, were creating miniature worlds for themselves in the form of clubs. The most prestigious club was the New England Women's Club, founded by Julia Ward Howe, author of the "Battle Hymn of the Republic" and a woman of enormous learning. Harriet was flattered when she was asked to join, but soon found it too full of "do's" and "don'ts" and cliques.

Harriet and Hattie decided to form a local club in Malden. They called it the Old and New, since they discussed ancient and modern topics and had both younger and older women. Harriet insisted that leadership be rotated among the members, and she encouraged self-education. As in the improvement circles of her youth, all shy women were given pep talks. Harriet would hear women say "Oh, I can't do anything," or "I don't amount to anything" when she tried to induce them to start to do creative writing. She would say things like, "You don't know what you can do until you try. *Do* try!" As a representative of the Old and New, Harriet served on the advisory committee of the General Federation of Women's Clubs founded in 1890.

Hattie taught a Boston Political Class, which the Nationals had helped to found. Social topics of all varieties were discussed freely. One of the discussion questions was: "Are laborers justified in striking to get higher wages?" Hattie became a specialist on the rules of conducting meetings. She taught on the subject and later wrote what would become a standard text, *Woman's Manual of Parliamentary Law.*

Harriet, like Lucy Larcom, was continually requested in her later years to lecture on her experiences as a mill worker. In the winter of 1881, she was invited to speak to the Lowell mill girls themselves— the new generation. Two hundred women came to

Harriet at 68 in 1893.

hear her in the hall of Lowell's People's Club. After her talk was over, Harriet was surrounded by people asking her questions about the old days. How had the mill girls of the thirties and forties found the time and energy to study and write?

"We work so hard and tend so much machinery, we are completely tired out by the end of the day," they told her. Instead of the look of zest and enthusiasm she remembered having seen on her contemporaries, these operatives wore expressions of hopelessness and seemed drained.

"The wages of these operatives are much lower," Harriet commented, "and although the hours of labor are less, they are obliged to do a far greater amount of work in a given time. They tend so many looms and frames that they have no time to think. They are always on the jump." She appealed to the new employers to be more like their earlier counterparts, at least as she remembered them, and to "mix a little conscience with their capital."

Harriet had a fuller life than her friend Lucy Larcom. Once she had told Lucy that because she was an unmarried woman she was "an undeveloped person." Yet when Harriet was only thirty-five, she saw that most of her adult years would be spent in housekeeping and mothering. She wrote a poem about this in which she symbolically gave up "men's applause, my dreams of high renown." Even when she had accomplished so much as a mature woman in the suffrage struggle, she felt she had missed out in some way. At seventy-three she wrote, "O there is so much that I wanted to do, so much that I might have done. If I had stuck to one thing [as Lucy Larcom] did I might have done better work in one line at least."

Harriet must have envied Lucy her immense reader popularity. But hers was a different kind of contribution. People like Harriet and Sarah Bagley gave the best part of themselves to moving history forward. Their lives were not safe ones. They submitted themselves to indignities and scorn to participate in uphill struggles.

If she did nothing else, she left behind her a valuable record of her life in her many diaries and scrapbooks, and etched a picture of "life among the early mill girls" in her *Loom and Spindle* that would serve as raw material for many scholars and readers.

Always referred to in her lifetime as "the widow of Warrington" or "the friend of Lucy Larcom," she was honored in her own right in the twentieth century. During the Bicentennial year of 1976, the Malden house of Harriet Hanson Robinson was declared a landmark.

BOOK THREE

Sarah G. Bagley

b. 1806

1

No Turnouts Need Apply

IT IS a day in early spring, 1846. An overseer calls over one of the weavers to where he is sitting. She is a slender young woman with a braid wound around her head. He sits in a chair on a raised platform, as if surveying his empire. In the weave room over 100 operatives are tending twice as many looms, repairing broken threads and replacing bobbins in the long shuttles, which race with incredible noise and speed back and forth between the warp threads.

"You belong to this . . . ah . . . female association, do you not?" the overseer asks.

"The Female Labor Reform Association is the name, sir," the young woman says, looking at him boldly.

"Well, Charlotte, I often see you passing notices and petitions here to all the girls."

"And the men, also," Charlotte answers, without insolence.

The man's face turns pink as he glowers at her. "This will not do. This will *not* do," he says in a threatening voice, and then more loudly, "For past offenses I shall declare a truce. But a repetition in any form of this behavior, and the corporation will punish you. I am speaking of a *dis*honorable discharge."

Sarah Bagley reported this incident in the *Voice of Industry*, a labor newspaper read all over New England, with phrases that will be repeated and remembered. For the month of May, Sarah had served as chief editor, since William Young, the publisher and editor had been ill. In taking on the job she had told her readers, "What we lack in editorial ability, in rhetorick, or historical research, be assured we will make up in heart."

Now, in her first editorial, she attacked the overseer who had threatened the weaver with dismissal:

> *What! Deprive us after working thirteen hours, the poor privilege of finding fault—of saying our lot is a hard one. Intentionally turn away a girl unjustly—persecute her for free expression of honest political opinions! We will make the name of him who dares the act, stink with every wind, from all points of the compass. He shall be hissed in the streets, and all the cities in this widespread republic.*

"Our name is legion, though our oppression be great," Sarah goes on to say.

Who was this woman speaking for the workers whose "name is legion?"

In 1910, the historian John R. Commons compiled a nine-volume collection of documents of American industrial history. Volume eight contains "The first investigation of labor conditions, 1845" with testimony given by nine mill workers. One account begins: "Miss Sarah G. Bagley said she had worked in the Lowell mills eight years and a half, six and a half on the Hamilton Corporation, and two years on the Middlesex."

For a long while this 1845 account was the basis of most of what was known about Sarah Bagley. A century later, one scholar devoted many years to unearthing sketchy family lists and local records, which establish the bare facts of her life before and during her stay in Lowell. It is only by her dynamic and powerful writings in the Voice of Industry that Sarah comes alive as the exceptional woman she was: organizer of the Female Labor Reform Associations, one of the first woman labor editors and journalists, and, finally, the first woman telegraph operator in the country.

Sarah George Bagley was born in 1806, third of five children of Nathan and Rhoda Witham Bagley. She was brought up in the small New Hampshire town of Candia with its granite boulders looking like the ruins of ancient castles and its view of the majestic Monadnock mountains. Sarah's grandfather on her mother's side had fought bravely in the Revolutionary War, but left his family to fend for itself when the war was over while he went off to join a community of Shakers.

Nathan Bagley moved his family to Meredith Bridge (later Laconia), New Hampshire and for a time was involved in some way in cotton manufacture. He did so poorly financially that Sarah, listed in the country records as "spinster of Lowell," had to pay $371 from her earnings toward the mortgage on the family property in 1840. That sum represented half of her earnings over a three-year period and shows how heavily the families of the mill girls depended on their incomes.

The records of the Hamilton Corporation in Lowell show that Sarah had entered the weave room of Mill B on September 22, 1837. She was thirty-one years old. The year before over a thousand of the mill operatives had marched singing down the Lowell streets in the biggest "turnout," or strike, up until that time. But 1837 was a quiet year. It was a year of severe economic "panic" followed by a depression in which workers all over the country were losing jobs.

The very same month in 1837 that Sarah went to work as a weaver, Samuel F. B. Morse, inventor of the telegraph, quietly applied for a patent in Washington. It was not to be approved for a number of years. By that time Sarah's fate would be curiously tied to Morse's.

At the end of her first year Sarah was earning top weaver rates, about eighty cents a day, from which the price of board, $1.25 a week was removed. Her skill may have been acquired by working in one of New Hampshire's small mills.

Although she found the work wearisome, Sarah did not seem at first to be overly troubled by mill conditions. She became one of the fifty or so young women who contributed regularly to the *Lowell Offering*. In one of the early trial numbers Sarah had a piece called "The Pleasures of Factory Life." While those pleasures, she wrote, were like angel's visits, few in number, and while she found talking to a fellow worker in the mill most difficult, thanks to the roar of the machinery, how marvelous it all was. "Who can closely examine all the movements of this complicated curious machinery, and not be led to the reflection, that the mind is boundless. It can accomplish almost any thing on which it fixes its attention."

And as to the overseer, the later villain whose name would be made to "stink with every wind," Sarah, in 1840, described him in almost the same words as one would describe one's father or brother: "We are placed in the care of overseers who feel

*An overseer comes to the aid of
an operative in the weave room.*

under moral obligation to look after our interests; and, if we are sick, to acquaint themselves with our situation and wants."

Was the Sarah aged forty simply more experienced and worldly-wise than the Sarah of thirty-four? The truth was that Lowell itself was changing. The peaceful *Idyl of Work* that Lucy Larcom recalled

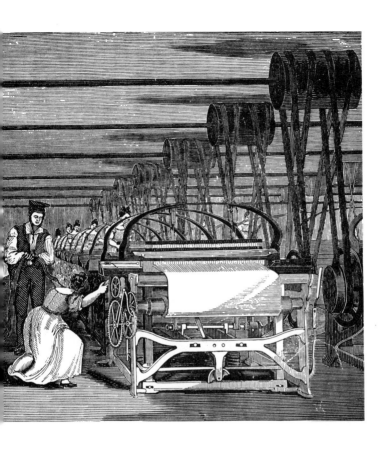

from her teenage years, even then far from an ideal, was becoming decidedly more grim. It was as if, once the mill owners had lured the young people from the countryside, they no longer had to make the situation attractive.

In the early years the townspeople could see the Merrimack River and the hills beyond, in the spaces between the mills. In time those spaces were filled up by more mills, until the barracks-like look of the red brick factory became a familiar New England sight. Five hundred Irish people, most of whom were day laborers working on the construction of the buildings, lived in sagging shanties built on the outskirts of town. Even the shiny new shops that had so much impressed Charles Dickens were replaced by rinky-dink stalls.

Experiments were tried with some of the weavers to get the most possible work out of them. A woman in Sarah's room was assigned two looms operating at

An experienced weaver teaches a new operative how to tend the looms.

a certain number of beats a minute. Another loom was added and the speed reduced. After some months, when she had gotten used to the extra loom, the speed was increased. This speedup resulted in very little extra earnings for the weaver, but considerably more cloth produced. In not many more decades weavers were tending as many as six looms.

And then there was the premium system. The premium was a bonus given to overseers and their assistants. It could amount to as much as two extra months' wages in a year. The overseer received his bonus when he could squeeze more work out of the operatives than other supervisors.

Sarah might find an overseer at her side suddenly sporting a nervous smile and offering to help her repair a thread. More likely the overseer would become disagreeable under pressure of the premium system. "Fly around and do your work!" one of them might snap. Or, "Sally and Dolly got off more pieces than you in the last four weeks. *They* come in before the power starts up in the morning, and if you don't get more done, I will send you off!" The girls began to refer to the overseer as "The Old Man," whispering about him in the boardinghouses and on the street, fearful of losing their jobs if they took any time off, or even relaxed at their posts.

A magazine in New Hampshire published the following "Definitions:"

Operative—a person who is employed in a factory, and who generally earns three times as much as he or she receives. Overseer—a servile tool in the hands of an agent, who will resort to the lowest, meanest and most grovelling measures to please his master, and to fill the coffers of the soulless corporation.

After three years as a weaver, Sarah changed over in the same mill to the dressing room. Work as a dresser did not pay as much, but Sarah had begun to feel worn out by the pace of the weave room. Both Lucy Larcom and Harriet Robinson had also chosen dressing room work at some point in their factory careers. The room was clean. The air was kept moist and warm for the dressing or starching of the warp threads, so any plants the girls put on the windowsills grew in tropical splendor. The dressing frame was a huge noisy affair and took some skill to manage. While Lucy had found it exasperating and had given up on it, Sarah considered it a challenge.

Lowell, the first large industrial city in the nation, became a center for scientific and technical development. In printing and dyeing fabric, in hydraulics and weaving, all new inventions were put to use.

In 1842, the Middlesex Corporation, a woolen mill, had installed the new Crompton loom. The new

The Middlesex Woolen Mills.

loom was capable of producing much more elaborate designs and could also turn out more fabric. At first the weavers at the Middlesex had been delighted, since the improvements would show up in their pay envelopes as more money. But their joy had not lasted long. A twenty percent wage cut was immediately announced. The *New York Tribune* had reported all this, saying that even with the wage cut the girls could earn "nearly as much." *Nearly* as much? That was not good enough. The newspaper had given the company's game away.

There was talk in the mill of another turnout. Pledges were taken from two hundred operatives who promised to join in. On the first day, seventy girls walked out. The Corporation did not wait for marches or speeches, but fired the seventy girls immediately. Those who applied for jobs at other mills in Lowell were told, "We don't want any of you turnouts from Middlesex." It was the old company "blacklist." Any operative leaving a mill with anything but a "regular discharge" could very likely not find employment anywhere in town, and sometimes the blacklist traveled ahead of her to other mill towns.

Sarah entered the weave room of the Middlesex several months after the unsuccessful strike. The record of Sarah's life is silent after this for two years. The cruel treatment of the seventy turnouts must have affected her deeply. Eighteen forty-two was a year of prosperity for the textile industry. But workers were actually putting in more hours in the 1840s than they had two decades earlier when the industry had begun. Even wicked England had a shorter work week than the New World utopia.

The hours of the operative were often compared to the hours of the farmer who then worked "from sun to sun." But while the people on the farm worked in the open air in tune to natural body needs, the operative worked in the close air of the mill. Windows were never opened, humidity was high and flying lint filled the air, particularly with the new and faster machinery. Bells punctuated every activity. The girls rose by the bell, entered the mill gates by the bell, were summoned to their half-hour lunches and back to the mills by bell. As the machinery speeded up the operatives began to feel like machines themselves. If turnouts were ineffective, other means would have to be found to move the "soulless corporations" to alter the growing degradation of the worker.

Sarah Bagley's hour was soon to come.

2

Try Again!

NO VOICE is wholly lost that is the voice of many men, an ancient philosopher said. Although the strikes and petitions of the first half of the nineteenth century seemed to have little effect, they brought workers together. By midcentury there was a mechanics and laborers' association in almost every industrial community.

In 1844, one of these issued a "call" for a convention of workers throughout New England. The call asked for "concerted measures to find a more excellent system of labor than that which has so long prevailed, and thus, under God, remove the heavy burdens which have long rested upon us and our children and let the oppressed go free."

There was a great deal of excitement in Lowell, which at that time had two workingmen's groups. It was a time when there were almost as many solutions to the problems of the worker as there were thinking men. When the convention finally took place in Boston in October of that year, there were, among the two hundred delegates, four distinct groups. Only two of the four appeared to have any grip on reality.

Firstly, there were the National Reformers who maintained that every adult was entitled to a piece of property equal to every other adult. Public lands would be given away in small amounts and whoever produced goods he and his family did not need, would barter such goods in the public square. George Henry Evans, the leader of the movement, promised that his plan would "reconstruct the map of the earth." No modest man, he!

Then there were the Associationists, who were influenced by the French thinker Charles Fourier. Fourier believed society should be organized into "phalanxes" or communes. Horace Greeley, the editor of the *New York Tribune*, had a regular column written by an Associationist in his newspaper, which helped make the idea popular.

There were forty Fourier-style communities in the United States in the 1840s. The most interesting of them was the nearby Brook Farm that the Lowell mill girls found so fascinating. Here some well-known intellectuals, among others, peeled carrots in the morning and read and discussed heavy ideas in the afternoons.

Thirdly, there were the Cooperators. Among the

more practical of the reformers, these people planned cooperative workshops to produce shoes, clothing, and even iron. A workingman's protective union actually set up consumer coops where products were sold at wholesale prices. The Cooperators' goal was to create a world where "every man shall feel that he is working for himself and not another."

A committee was formed to draw up a constitution for the body, from then to be called the New England Workingmen's Association (NEWA). Another convention would be held six months later in Lowell. Many resolutions were passed. Each one seemed equally forceful, but there was one, put forth by the fourth group of labor people that would be the spearhead for labor activity in the months to come. This was the resolution for the "Ten Hour System," suggesting petitions to the legislature asking for a ten-hour workday. In this struggle women workers were to play a crucial role.

December, 1844. It is a very cold night. Snow has been falling for hours and the Lowell streets look like a vast white desert. A group of women sit in a small dimly-lit room just outside the large room where Lowell's Mechanics and Laborers' Association meets.

This is the second meeting of the group. The first one had been adjourned because only twenty women had shown up and they were hoping for a larger turn-out the next time. Now it *is* the next time and, possibly because of the weather, there are only fifteen present.

"I suppose we must forgive our sisters," says one of them. She is young, perhaps no more than seventeen, and has a determined look about her. "I'm afraid threatenings and fears have taken hold of their minds."

"I don't suppose there is anything to be gained coming here on a night like this, except perhaps wet capes and chilblains," says another.

"There is something indeed to be gained," says a woman who appears to be in her late thirties. It is clear she will emerge as the leader of the group, since throughout the meeting all seem to look to her for guidance. "Any small thing we do to improve the condition of those with whom we are associated, improves our own condition as well," she continues. "The world cannot be moved in a day. More will gather around us in this holy cause. I'm sure that much good will come of our efforts."

"How then shall we proceed?" the younger woman asks.

"We must proceed exactly as if we were many. I suggest we set up two committees, one to draft a constitution and one to name officers."

"And we must have a motto. Something that will inspire us," the first woman says. There are a few moments of silence while people think.

"I am reminded of a spider who starts his web all

over again each time it is destroyed. Why not: 'Let's try again'?" someone suggests.

"*Try again* . . . *try again* . . . that's perfect." There is unanimous agreement on the motto.

Several planning meetings followed. The group originally intended to become the ladies' auxiliary to the men's group, but the group must have realized that if they did so, the tail would soon be wagging the horse. A new organization was formed, called the Lowell Female Labor Reform Association (FLRA). Of the fifteen who had been present at the first official meeting, thirteen were made officers! Sarah Bagley was chosen president.

When the New England Workingmen's Association held it's first convention, Sarah reported that the FLRA had grown to 304 members in its first three months. Sarah was elected corresponding secretary for the workingmen's organization. Perhaps the most historic thing about NEWA was that, for the first time anywhere, women were accepted on an equal footing with men.

Again the starry-eyed utopian reformers were on hand; also two leading antislavery leaders, Wendell Phillips and William Lloyd Garrison, who were sympathetic to labor struggles. Robert Owen, who had set up a model industrial community in Scotland, came to talk about his planned world convention, meant to "emancipate the human race from sin, misery, and all kinds of slavery." He hoped to attract capitalist and laborer alike to work out their mutual problems. As with similar schemes, the mill owners just failed to show up!

Sarah's speech was eloquent and direct. As she arose, several women from the FLRA came down the aisle with a beautifully painted banner reading: UNION FOR POWER—POWER TO BLESS HUMANITY. Talking about the frustrations of women workers who were fired and blacklisted for speaking out and who could not even vote to express their sentiments, she said:

> *For the last half century, it has been deemed a violation of woman's sphere to appear before the public as a speaker; but when our rights are trampled upon what shall we do but appeal to the people? Shall it be said again to the daughters of New England, that they have no political rights? It is for the working-men of this country to answer these questions —what shall we expect at your hands in the future?*

Sarah was counting on the men, who had the right to vote, to represent the interests of the women as well. But, she assured the men, they didn't expect to be soldiers in this war, since they were merely female.

They would help "like heroines of the Revolution" by bringing blankets to the front, or filling "their knapsacks from our pantries."

However maidenly Sarah's speech, it was a remarkable display of feeling and militancy. The next speaker thanked her for the group in a "feeling and appropriate manner," and began to speak in somewhat lofty terms about "woman's influence in the past."

The Lowell FLRA had six hundred members before the year was out. Women operatives in Waltham and Fall River in Massachusetts and in Manchester, Dover and Nashua in New Hampshire started branches of their own.

The groups became the center of social life in these towns. Parties not only made them more popular, but brought men and women together in a good cause. One of these took place on the eve of Saint Valentine's Day in 1846. There were visitors from mill towns in two states. Tables were loaded with "fruits of the earth and ingenious preparations of ladies' domestic arts." The Lowell Brass Band played and a male quartet, which included two schoolchildren, sang in harmony.

A booklet called *The Valentine Offering* had been printed for the occasion. Included in it were several pieces on the subject of love, including a rich man's marriage proposal. Describing himself as the son of a manufacturer, whose servants never speak to the family until spoken to, this young man declares himself "head and ears over in love" with the mill girl. The girl responds by saying she wouldn't dream of marrying a gentleman. "What could I do with a gentleman?" she asks. "I could not live on cigars and politics, and dance the rest of the time." What was more, she would not consider being "an idle drone, living on the hard-earned goods of the worthy laborer." She rejects him roundly.

A "Valentine Post Office," set up on a lower floor of city hall, where the party was held, yielded an anonymous poem:

> But, if I must wend my way,
>   Uncheered by hope's sweet song,
> God grant, that in the mills, a day
>   May be but "Ten Hours" long.

Among the speakers was a certain John C. Cluer, an English weaver newly arrived in the United States, who could hold audiences spellbound. His humor was edged with politics and his politics with humor. He was Sarah's right-hand man.

Bagley and Cluer presided over a huge meeting in Manchester. One thousand were in the audience, two-thirds of them women. Cluer addressed the crowd for three hours on "The Ten Hour System and Factory Oppression." The applause was thundering, the women waving muffs and handkerchiefs in the air.

Afterward the group divided in two. The men met to form a Mechanics and Laborers' Association, and the woman to create an FLRA wing. The group would soon be the size of Lowell's. Sarah spoke with "candor, truthfulness and beauty" and presented a constitution modeled on the Lowell FLRA's. It was adopted without any changes.

A letter of congratulations to the new group appeared in the *Manchester Democrat* written by a Lowell member. "Let us encourage and strengthen each other in every good word and work," it said, and went on:

> *If discouragements rise as they surely will, will you yield to despair and falter? God forbid! Rather take the motto of your sister Association of Lowell, and let its spirit fire your every heart with* NEW ZEAL *and unwavering hope—*"We'll try again!"

A smaller group turned out to hear the two organizers in Fitchburg, Massachusetts. The two dozen women had waded through knee-high drifts of snow to hear them. When Bagley and Cluer returned to Lowell, they found a letter from the Fitchburg operatives saying that "if Miss Bagley or some of the Society in Lowell come up with Mr. Cluer next time he comes, they will form a society."

Cluer's usefulness to the ten-hour movement would soon make him the target of a vicious attack.

3

Labor Hearing or Sellout?

THE MOTTO "Try again!" turned out to be more useful than the women imagined when they created it. The ten-hour struggle was uphill all the way. It started with the petitions to the Massachusetts legislature from the beginning of the 1840s. The female operatives in all the mill towns were the most outspoken, spurred on by Sarah Bagley's energy and leadership.

It was more than two decades since the first power looms were put into motion, but the hours now were longer than they had been at the beginning. The "lighting up" system had begun, so that the workers could be kept at their posts when daylight was not available. As one of the factory magazines commented, "ten years ago the corporations would not have dared to propose to the girls to work by lamplight in the morning and evening, and we trust the girls in every mill in New England will rise up against this outrageous custom."

The petitions argued that a ten-hour law would add to the length of the workers' lives and give them time to tend to their personal affairs and their "mental and moral cultivation."

A long scroll with two thousand names, fifteen hundred from Lowell, had been presented to the Massachusetts legislature early in 1845. The four names at the head of the list included Sarah Bagley's. The most eloquent of all the petitions, it read:

> We the undersigned peaceable, industrious and hardworking men and women of Lowell, in view of our condition—the evils already come upon us by toiling from thirteen to fourteen hours per day, confined in unhealthy apartments, exposed to the poisonous contagion of air, vegetable, animal and mineral properties, debarred from proper physical exercise, mental discipline and mastication cruelly limited, and thereby hastening us on through pain, disease and privation, down to a premature grave, pray the legislature to institute a ten-hour working day in all the factories of the state.

The petitions were becoming a positive nuisance to the legislature. It could no longer postpone taking some action. Like a sleepy bear, it had lifted its head

and blinked its eyes, appointed a committee on manufactures to look into the matter, and then hoped the
women operatives would be too shy to show up. "I
would inform you," the response said, "that as the
greater part of the petitioners are females, it will be
necessary for them to make the defence, or we shall
be under the necessity to set it aside."

The response was signed: William Schouler. To
many of the operatives this name rang a bell. It was
the same Schouler who was the editor and publisher
of the *Lowell Courier* and who for two years had
funded the *Lowell Offering*. The habit of his junior
editor, William Robinson, of speaking openly and
forthrightly about the evils of slavery, had made him
most uncomfortable. Most citizens of Lowell knew
that he had been elected to the Massachusetts House
of Representatives, but why had he suddenly been appointed chairman of this rather important committee?
The group was renamed Special Committee to Inves-
tigate Labor Conditions. It was the first of its kind in
the history of the country.

Schouler had judged the petitioners wrong.
There was no shyness among them at all. Sarah wrote
a note to Schouler in the name of the body: "We hold
ourselves in readiness to defend the petitions referred
to at any time when you will grant us a hearing."

Nine operatives were chosen to testify at that
hearing. Of the nine, six were women. Sarah's name

had not, at first, been on the list, but when two of the women chosen could not be found, Sarah became one of the replacements.

What we know of the hearing comes down to us in the Commonwealth of Massachusetts Report, House Document No. 50. The document has the ring of truth as one reads the testimony of one witness after another. But when it was published, Sarah was furious and wrote a piece for the *Voice of Industry* entitled, "What Was Omitted in the Report."

"I am not prepared to state that there is not *one* original sentence, but I am prepared to say that whatever was given, was so changed in its connection, or removed from its original position, that it *was* made to say what we never said, or thought of saying." Using the report and Sarah's corrections, we reconstruct it to the best of our ability here. . . .

February 13, 1845. Eliza Hemingway, a young operative, wearing her best Sabbath dress, steps forward when her name is called and sits in the chair placed in front of the room for the witnesses. She looks directly into the eyes of the committee's questioner, but speaks only in response to a question and gives only the information that seems to be required.

Eliza has worked in the Lowell mills for three years, she testifies. She starts work at five in the morning and works until seven at night. She has counted the number of lamps used in the weave room before sunrise and after sunset. There are 293 small ones and sixty-one large ones. One hundred fifty work in this close air. There are never fewer than six people out sick at any one time, sometimes as many as thirty. She has often had to spend days in her boardinghouse room nursing a chest ailment or general malaise. Most of the girls did not stay in the mills more than three years. There is, says Eliza, a very strong desire among the women she has spoken to, to have a ten-hour day.

Eliza Hemingway rises and Judith Payne takes her place. She is an older woman, her hair drawn in a severe bun behind her head. She is also, she says, a weaver. The previous payday she received $14.66 for five weeks' work, not counting her room and board, which is paid directly to the boardinghouse keeper. She came to Lowell sixteen years ago. After working only one year, she became so ill she had to go to her home to rest. She stayed away from the mills seven years, being sick most of that time. Now she has been in the mills seven additional years. She has been sick a good bit of the time, having lost about a year's worth of pay. She thinks the illness comes from her long hours of labor each day, the short time given to eat and digest the two meals a day and the bad air in the

A "tintype" taken in the 1860s, showing two weavers in work dresses holding the shuttles from their looms.

weave room. All women she works with, says Judith, favor the ten-hour system.

Now it is Sarah Bagley's turn. She looks warily at the questioner and answers each question at some length. Her testimony is the longest. It is nine years since she came to Lowell. After only three years, her health began to fail. She returns to her mountain home in New Hampshire six weeks every summer, mainly to rest. In spite of this vacation she missed a third of a year's work the previous year because of sickness. The worst of the evils, Sarah tells the committee, is the shortness of time allowed for meals. The next is the length of the working day. There is no time to tend to one's simplest needs, and no time to cultivate one's mind.

"How do you know," the questioner asks, "if the operatives would spend the extra time, if it should be given to them, in the cultivation of their minds?"

"A great many of them would," Sarah says confidently.

"You seem to be so sure that these girls want to improve their mental capacities. What evidence do you have?"

"Well, for one, many of the operatives who have difficulty in the simple branches of education come to my sleeping apartment. I write letters for them and instruct them, without any compensation. I simply want to help the more unfortunate members of the

class from which I come." Most of the girls had a high
moral and intellectual character, Sarah adds. Many
taught Sunday school and many attended lyceum lectures and classes with the last shred of energy left to
them, after a weary day at the spindles and looms.
(This is the way the committee reported the exchange
between the questioner and Sarah Bagley: "Miss Bagley said she had kept evening school during the winter
months, for four years and thought that this extra
labor must have injured her health.")

There is a bit of drama when a mechanic in the
Lawrence mill comes forward to give testimony.

"Are you Mr. Herman Abbott?"

"Yes, sir," says the man, looking down at the
floor.

"How long have you been working for the Lawrence Corporation?"

"Thirteen years, sir." Now he looks up and seems
to be gathering his forces.

"When you talk with the female operatives, Mr.
Abbott, do you hear much complaining?" asks the
questioner.

"Never heard much complaint among the girls,
not about the long hours any way. The subject is
never spoken of. The girls know that if they work only
ten hours, their wages would be reduced in propor-
tion."

At this point someone in the labor group asks

Schouler's permission to put a question to Abbott. Schouler nods hesitantly and frowns.

"Mr. Abbott," asks the labor man, "Did you have an interview with Mr. Aiken, the agent of your mill, after you were notified to come here as a witness?"

Schouler jumps up and says to Abbott, "DO NOT ANSWER THAT QUESTION!" Then, composing himself, turns to the other members of the committee to explain his action. "Don't you see," he says, "they are trying to implicate this man?"

"Of *course* we are trying to implicate Mr. Abbott," says the labor man. "The truth exists. Either he tells us all of it, or his testimony is worth nothing." The committee confers for a few minutes and then overrules Mr. Schouler and orders Mr. Abbott to answer the labor people's question.

"Yes, I did speak with Mr. Aiken," Abbott says, looking at his shoes again.

"And what did Mr. Aiken tell you?"

"He said, 'You must go, but you must *say as little as possible.*' " (None of this was reported on the official record.)

The committee, after the hearing, had gone through the motions of an extensive on-the-spot investigation. On the first of March they had taken the one-hour railroad trip from Boston to Lowell. They visited several of the mills and asked many questions.

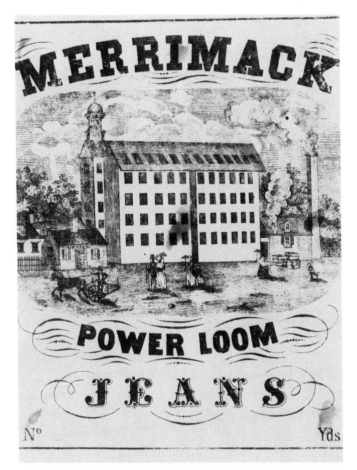

Another cloth label from the Merrimack Mills.

They had reported the mills "neat and clean," well landscaped, with trim squares of lawn and planted trees. In the mills they had been delighted to find the "shrubs and plants, such as geraniums, roses and numerous varieties of cactus" that the girls had nurtured on the windowsills. If a girl had time to grow flowers in the mill, how overworked could she be?

As far as the way the girls *looked*, well, anyone could see that they were "healthy and robust" as any girls who lived in the country were. And, as everyone knew, these farmers' daughters would stay in the mills only until they had "laid by a few hundred dollars." Then they would play out the feminine role and "get married, settle down in life, and become heads of families."

So why any labor laws at all?

The Committee had simply wanted to get off the hook or "be discharged from the further consideration of the matters referred to them." They felt that in America labor and captial were "on an equality" and did not need legislators to intervene. The Massachusetts legislature would not move one inch until labor groups and reformers had "tried again" many times over.

The more liberal newspapers had been as outraged by the committee's report as the operatives were. The *Lowell Advertiser* said, "Is it the business of the legislature to pass laws only for corporations, and not for those whose labor makes the corporations valuable?" Sarah Bagley's comment was, "If they gave the operatives the same protection they gave to animals, our condition would be greatly improved."

The Female Labor Reform Association of Lowell had held a meeting on April 1. Resolutions were passed lamenting "the lack of independence, honesty and humanity" of the house committee. As to William Schouler, the "corporation tool," the girls said: "We will use our best endeavors and influence to keep him in the 'city of spindles,' where he belongs, and not trouble Boston folks with him."

They were referring to the elections to come the following November. That year a curious thing happened. As a result of the influence of women, who were not legally allowed to vote, an influential newspaper editor and publisher was defeated in his bid for a legislative seat. It would not soon be forgotten.

4

The Cluer Scandal

SCHOULER would not let the "Female Association" get away with this strategy. How he could retaliate was the question. To attack Sarah Bagley was like attacking the Virgin Mary, and then he would have to deal with the most articulate tongue and pen in the ten-hour movement.

The weak link, as he discovered, was John C. Cluer. Cluer had lived in New York before coming to Lowell, and Schouler was able to find several unsavory characters from Cluer's past in England to smear him.

Schouler mounted his campaign slowly, first working on the image of Cluer as a troublemaker. "His talent is to denounce and pull down," he wrote in the *Courier*. "He stirs up bad blood between the employed and the employer." He challenged Cluer to come up with a "practical plan," instead of stirring people up. Cluer in a speech in front of the Third Universalist Church outlined a fairly moderate plan involving capital and labor. The *Courier* did not report a word of this speech.

Cluer invited Schouler to debate him openly and called a meeting at Lowell's city hall. When Cluer arrived at the hall, the man in charge was telling everyone, "Go home—there is no meeting here tonight."

The battle continued in the press. Schouler called Cluer a "mountebank." Cluer called Schouler "a child in intellect" and accused him of "meanness, duplicity, servility, double-mindedness and treachery." Schouler, he wrote in the *Voice*, was being hired by vampires to drain the blood of the "sons and daughters of Toil."

Now began the "letters" from New York, in almost every issue of the *Courier*, revealing the "facts" about John Cluer's past life. He was a bigamist, the letters said, having married his second wife without divorcing his first. Although he was a temperance lecturer, he had been an alcoholic, was arrested when in New York and used an assumed name at one time or another. Worst of all, Schouler revealed that Cluer had been with the Chartist labor movement in Great Britain.

Like the labor reformers in the United States, the Chartists made demands that any reasonable society today would grant as humane. In fact, the Chartist demands became law in Great Britain eventually. But, like all reformers, they were depicted in the conservative press as rabble rousers and rioters.

Being a Chartist had been only a small part of Cluer's career. Just what the rest of his life was like became of some interest to the *Voice of Industry*, which dispatched an editor to go to New York and do some detective work. They discovered that at least one of the letters to the *Courier* had been written *for* the man who signed it, and even used a wrong first name! The life they pieced together, finally, was not one any person would feel ashamed of.

As a boy Cluer had been apprenticed to a hand loom weaver. Having gotten some acting training from a roving theater group, Cluer found that whatever he chose to speak about would move his audiences. After making some rousing speeches for temperance, he was persuaded by a group of fellow weavers to speak for them and he began to negotiate for the weavers in their dealings with their employers.

At seventeen, Cluer found himself married to a woman who lived across the street from him. The woman had a bad reputation and did not treat him well. Still he tried, under the influence of his mother, to make a go of it. Finally he drifted away and fell in love with a fellow temperance worker, whom he "married." Getting divorced in Britain involved huge sums of money and most working-class people ignored the law. So "bigamy" of the sort Cluer practiced was very common. His arrest in New York had to do with a political speech and not with any criminal activity.

While the investigation was going on, Cluer defended himself in the pages of the Voice as best he could. The attacks continued. Once, when he went to speak to the Manchester operatives, he found an evil-looking man sitting in the front row. The man handed him a note threatening violence to his person if he did not "take another course."

"The capitalists and their press, aided by British villains, hunt me like bloodhounds," he wrote. "They have money and at present they do not spare it in order to crush me, but it is not *me* they care about, it is the cause I am engaged in."

Sarah could do nothing about this except mobilize the operatives in Cluer's defense. At a joint meeting of the male and female associations in Lowell, resolutions were passed that were later printed in the Voice:

Resolved, That the character of J. C. Cluer so far as the investigation has been made, has proved better than our most sanguine expectations could have anticipated.

Resolved, That the attack made upon Mr.
Cluer was intended to destroy, through him,
the Labor Reform movement; but in this
also, the enemies of all true liberty have been
completely foiled. May the time never come
when the reformers of labor shall be so
indolent as not to disturb the watchdogs of
the corporations.

The Fourth of July was one of the four paid holidays the mill workers enjoyed. With the American Revolution fresh in their minds, the workers made much of this celebration. The word "revolution" still had some respectability and the language of that conflict was constantly used. Mill owners were referred to as "aristocracy," female operatives as "daughters of America." The 1845 July Fourth event was a picnic in a large park in Woburn, Massachusetts. The New England Workingmen's Association and the Female Labor Reform Associations were at the height of their popularity.

Hundreds of workers began to arrive at about ten in the morning, coming by stagecoach and railroad. The Lowell group marched from the railroad station to the park with a brass band leading the way.

At ten-thirty, a committee was appointed to choose officers for NEWA. Sarah Bagley was chosen one of the five vice-presidents. The speech Sarah was to make created a considerable sensation, although she claimed afterward that it had not been prepared.

Someone who heard her said that people were so quiet one could actually hear the rustling of the leaves when Sarah paused for breath. "She spoke of the *Lowell Offering*," the *Voice* report said, "that it was not the voice of the operatives—it gave a false representation of the truth—it was controlled by the manufacturing interest to give a gloss to their inhumanity." Anything written for the *Offering* that was critical of conditions was found unsuitable for publication. The operatives, she said, were "doomed to eternal slavery" and deprived of the most human comforts. As to the hours of labor, they were longer than ever. But the girls had united to do something about this and now had a flourishing society in Lowell of five hundred members. "She took her seat amidst the loud and unanimous huzzas of the deep moved throng," concluded the report.

Harriet Farley, the chief editor of the *Offering*, took Sarah's remarks as a personal insult. In the conservative *Lowell Courier* and the more liberal *Lowell Advertiser*, the two women exchanged letters that became increasingly heated. Like the Cluer-Schouler battle, it had the whole town talking.

The *Offering* had not given a completely one-sided picture of life in the textile mills, but, as was

the custom of the day, there was usually a happy ending tacked on to any story showing the workers' mis-
eries. The editorials advised its women readers to play
the traditional woman's role of being "submissive,
cheerful and contented," and to "remain entirely neutral in political and economic matters." The operatives
demonstrated that the *Offering* was no longer meeting
their needs by dropping their subscriptions. The kind
of attack that Sarah made could be a final blow and it
was her awareness of this that made Farley reply sar-
castically, thereby giving Sarah only more fuel for the
flame.

Said Bagley: "We wish to have the *Offering*
stand upon its own bottom, instead of going out as the
united voice of the Lowell operatives, while it wears
the corporation lock and their apologizers hold the
key. We have not written this article to evince that
there is 'mind among the spindles,' but to show that
the minds here are not *all spindles.*"

Said Farley: "I cannot do all the things that she
can, for I cannot make a speech or talk politics, or
speak of the factory system as she represents it, for it
never seemed to me a 'durance vile,' or Inquisition
torture, or slave-driven task work. I never felt dis-
posed to croak or whine about my factory life and
have endeavored to impose a cheerful spirit into the
little magazine I edit."

Said Bagley: "I notice by the *Advertiser* of last

week that I have been *favored* with a specimen of *refined* literature, from the pen of one of the *geniuses* of the age. Have the columns of the *Offering* ever contended against oppression or abuse in any form? If so, I would like to read the number containing such an article; not because I *want* such facts to exist, but because they do exist and should not go unrebuked."

Finally, when Bagley called Farley "a mouthpiece of the corporations," Farley retired from the word war.

But soon Farley had Sarah on her own turf. Sarah was invited to the *Offering*'s improvement circle meeting. There Farley took the floor and held it, insisting that she had never rejected a controversial piece and that she had it on good authority that her predecessor, Reverend Thomas, had not either. They had simply, she said, turned away *badly written* articles.

At this point Sarah waved an article she had been holding in her hand, saying that she had with her one of the rejected pieces and wanted to read it to the group. Farley commanded her to be silent and continued with her talk.

But, as Sarah had said in one of her newspaper pieces, "*She* has literary talents to which *I* lay no claim; but I have *facts*." And the facts were that the *Offering*, by 1845, had only fifty-two subscribers left. Agents of the corporations were taking multiple copies to keep the magazine afloat, and one of the companies had even purchased one thousand dollars worth of back issues.

The *Offering* went under at the end of 1845. That year the *Voice of Industry* had absorbed two other labor newspapers and moved its base from Fitchburg to Lowell. This brought it closer to the center of Female Labor Reform Association activity and enabled Sarah to serve on the publishing committee along with editor William F. Young and Joel Hatch, the man who had done the investigation of John Cluer. For several issues, when Young was ill, Sarah served as chief editor, promising her readers to make up in enthusiasm what she might lack in education. "Our heart, yea, our whole soul, is wrapped up in the cause of the oppressed, of the downtrodden millions throughout the world," she wrote. In 1846, the *Voice's* peak year, it would have two thousand subscribers and truly be the voice of the working people.

5

As Is Woman,
So Is the Race

THE *Voice* did a great deal to publicize the activities of the Female Labor Reform Association and the association, in turn, took the newspaper into the mills and solicited subscriptions.

One of the great successes of the Lowell Association was the Industrial Reform Lyceum. While the mill girls were enthusiastic lecture-goers there were not too many places where they could hear reformers speaking their minds. Here was the earliest discussion of women's rights in the country. One announcement invited all people interested in the welfare "of the producing classes" to come to a talk on the theme "that the disfranchisement of woman is a flagrant violation of her natural and inalienable rights and the fruitful source of innumerable social and political evils."

Antislavery speeches of people like William Lloyd Garrison fired the operatives to sign abolition petitions by the hundreds. It was said that if you lined up all the people signing one of those petitions, the line would stretch a mile!

Articles that the *Lowell Offering* had found too controversial were printed up, along with new material in a series of pamphlets called *Factory Tracts*. Labor reform groups helped the association distribute these tracts in several cities in the Northeast. Some of the articles parodied *Offering* titles; "The Evils of Factory Life" was one; "Some of the Beauties of Our Factory System—Otherwise, Lowell Slavery" was another.

What had made the Lowell "factory system" so famous the world over was the seeming interest taken by the mill owners in the young women placed into their care by anxious families. In the early, more leisurely days some of the mill personnel had indeed acted in a fatherly fashion.

But much of the so-called "paternalism" of the mill owners was actually the way the mill girls looked after themselves, since they were the typically "vir-

Regulations for the Middlesex Woolen Mills, 1846. Note that the operatives had to pledge themselves to a year's work and give two weeks notice, but the corporations could fire them at will with no notice.

REGULATIONS

TO BE OBSERVED BY ALL PERSONS EMPLOYED IN THE FACTORIES OF THE

MIDDLESEX COMPANY.

The overseers are to be punctually in their rooms at the starting of the mill, and not to be absent unnecessarily during working hours. They are to see that all those employed in their rooms are in their places in due season. They may grant leave of absence to those employed under them, when there are spare hands in the room to supply their places; otherwise they are not to grant leave of absence, except in cases of absolute necessity. Every overseer must be the last to leave the room at night, and must see that the lights are all properly extinguished, and that there is no fire in the room. No overseer should leave his room in the evening while the mill is running, except in case of absolute necessity.

All persons in the employ of the Middlesex Company are required to observe the regulations of the overseer of the room where they are employed. They are not to be absent from their work, without his consent, except in case of sickness, and then they are to send him word of the cause of their absence.

They are to board in one of the boarding-houses belonging to the Company, unless otherwise permitted by the agent or superintendent, and conform to the regulations of the house where they board. They are to give information at the counting-room of the place where they board when they begin; and also give notice whenever they change their boarding place.

The Company will not employ any one who is habitually absent from public worship on the Sabbath, or whose habits are not regular and correct.

All persons entering into the employment of the Company are considered as engaged for twelve months; and those who leave sooner will not receive a regular discharge.

All persons intending to leave the employment of the Company are to give two weeks' notice of their intention to their overseer; and their engagement is not considered as fulfilled unless they comply with this regulation.

Smoking within the factory yards will in no case be permitted.

The pay-roll will be made up to the end of every month, and the payment made in the course of the following week.

These regulations are considered a part of the contract with persons entering into the employment of the MIDDLESEX COMPANY.

Samuel Lawrence, *Agent.*

Lowell, July 1, 1846.

Joel Taylor, Printer, Courier Office.

tuous" and earnest products of their Victorian up-
bringing. And some of it was a kind of policing of the
population and was resented.

The tracts show the new "hand" getting her regulation paper in the counting room of the mill, sur-
prised to find she must commit her labor for a year
to the first mill she has chosen. Likewise she is forced
to live in the company boardinghouse, locked into a
fourteen-by-sixteen-foot room with at least five other
women "with all the trunks and boxes necessary to
their convenience." Her free time is not truly her own
for she must be in her room by ten o'clock and "her
footsteps dogged to see that they do not stray beyond
the corporation limits."

Now the new hand finds she must be at the loom
at the stroke of five o'clock in the morning, or pay a
penalty for lateness. Two hastily-gulped meals in the
half hour allotted to her to get from the mill to the
boardinghouse and back, bring her to the closing time
of seven o'clock at night, or seven-ten, if the clocks had
been made to play tricks, as they sometimes were.

Pew rent for church is taken out of the operative's wages and the regulations require that she attend some church. But the owners have no hesitation
in hiring day laborers to do construction work on the
Sabbath, with the result that the noise of several dozen
men splitting logs and blasting rock makes it difficult
for the churchgoer to worship.

Only "ignorance, misery, and *premature decay* of both *body* and *intellect*" could result from such a way of living, said the tracts. Soon the country would consist of "one great hospital" filled with factory workers and their sister slaves from the South.

For those who ask "How shall we act?" under those circumstances, the pamphlet said:

We answer there is in this city an Association called the Female Labor Reform Association, having for its professed object, the amelioration of the condition of the operative. In the strength of our united influence we will soon show these drivelling *cotton lords, this mushroom aristocracy of New England, who so arrogantly aspire to lord it over God's heritage, that our rights cannot be trampled upon with impunity.*

No doubt Sarah Bagley had an intimate hand in the preparation of the *Factory Tracts,* but since her name appeared on none of the articles, she evidently made her contribution as an editor. In March, 1846, the Female Labor Reform Association became the owner of the *Voice of Industry.* The paper was listed as part of Sarah's "personal estate," and she was the one who officially paid the taxes for it.

VOICE OF INDUSTRY.

ORGAN OF THE NEW ENGLAND WORKINGMEN'S ASSOCIATION.

GAGE & CLO

W. F. YOUNG, Editor.

LOWELL, MASS., FRIDAY MORNING, MAY 1, 1846.

VOICE OF INDUSTRY,
PUBLISHED EVERY FRIDAY,
At No. 38. CENTRAL ST., LOWELL, MASS.
BY THE
N. E. WORKINGMEN'S ASSOCIATION.

J. S. FLETCHER, } Publishers
SARAH G. BAGLEY, } Committee.
JOEL HAYDN, }

TERMS—$1.00 In Advance.
☞ All Communications should be directed (post paid,) to the Office of Industry.

Poetry.

From the New York Tribune.
Gentle Words—A Song.
BY C. D. STUART.

A young Rose in the Summer time
Is beautiful to me,
And glorious the many stars,
That glimmer on the Sea;
But Gentle Words and loving hearts,
And hands to clasp my own,
Are better than the brightest flowers
Or Stars that ever shone!

The sun may warm the grass to life,
The dew the drooping flower;
And eyes grow bright that watch the light
Of Autumn's opening hour;
But words that breathe of tenderness,
And smiles we know are true,
Are warmer than the summer time,
And brighter than the dew.

It is not much the world can give,
With all its subtle art,
And gold and gems are not the things
To satisfy the Heart;
But, oh, if those who cluster 'round
The altar and the hearth,
Have gentle words and loving smiles,

his plans of revenge were about to be execut-
ed; 'twas the smile of a fiend, as he saw his
victim almost within his grasp.

Wequash, who had made proposals of marriage to Chantayvra, the beautiful daughter of
Monomotto, a powerful sachem of the same
tribe. When with all the dignity of a warrior,
he stood in her presence, and solicited her
hand, how did the dark passions of the Indian's heart thirst for revenge when told, in her
firm but simple language, "she loved another."
In silence he left her presence, but well knew
the maiden, what that silence indicated ; and
oh, how her heart beat with fear for its beloved object. Well did she know that sleep
would scarce be given to his eyelids, or rest to
his limbs, till he was revenged on his hated,
because more successful rival. 'Twas the silence of the calm that precedes the fearful tem-
pest. That rival was Oneactah, the son of one
of the principal chiefs of the tribe—a warrior
of tried courage; in war he was foremost, and
his fleetness in the chase none questioned.
Worthy was he of the beautiful Chantayvra,
or, as she was known in the tribe, "The Flower of the Forest."

But return we to Wequash, whom we left
under the "Old Oak Tree," at the base of the
eastern ridge. He at length prepared to depart. Twilight had cast her brown mantle
over the valley, when, after adjusting his
weapons with great care, he entered a thicket
of junipers, at the foot of the hill, and placing
his hands to his mouth in a peculiar manner,
sent forth an imitation of the whip-poor-will's
note. Directly was heard an answering note
coming from the hill-top, which was covered

that one by one looked forth from the clear
blue vault upon the gay scene.

But return all the dancers around the con-
vival fire, they only attracted particular attention. They were indeed a noble pair. The
maiden's costume was rich, even for an Indian
bride, for this was the marriage festival of Oneactah and Chantayvra, and they were the
couple towards whom all eyes were directed.

Chantayvra's jet, unconfined as black as
the raven, descended to her waist, at which
place the braids were gathered up in a seemingly careless manner, by an ivory or bone
clasp of curious workmanship. Her head-
dress consisted of three magnificent eagle
plumes, confined to a band of feathers skil-
fully wrought, which clasped her forehead,
and prevented her dark tresses from conceal-
ing a high intellectual brow, of a beautiful
copper color. A gray cotton shawl, the proba-
ble plunder of some predatory excursion a-
mong the whites, was thrown about her form,
the very beau ideal of beauty, symmetry and
loveliness, and bound around her waist by a
rich belt of wampum, to which was also suspended a short skirt of purple cloth ornament-
ed with Indian figures and devices. Her moc-
casins were likewise beautifully worked and
enriched with beads of various colors, among
which the variegated plumage of the forest
birds was ingeniously interwoven. Her teeth,
as she smiled, were white and regular, and
her eyes, so bright yet melting, rivalled the
sweet gazelle's in the liquid softness of
their expression; these, with her voice, which
"was low and soft, an excellent thing in woman," and the ever varying expression of her

towards it. Even the old ...
their peril, yet none les...
grew pale, nor a lip qui...
noiselessly to the attack ;
breath, and clenched teet...
um showed a firmness t...
could subdue. When at...
the palisades they were d...
nel, who roared out w...
"Owanux! Owanux!" (E...
nux!) O, what a thrillin...
"Advance! Advance! ...
"Owanux! Owanux!" res...
ing breeze from the fort, ...
astonishment and rage. ...
troops over the walls of ...
Indians were rallying, po...
destructive fire ; then th...
muskets, rushed upon th...
"Shelter'd by their wig...
by their sachems and w...
made a powerful resistan...
anzu attacked the Engl...
window attacked the Eng...
that would have done b...
Where the fight raged thi...
the black plume of Onea...
raven over the battle-fi...
a feeling such as despe...
dneey,—he fought for a ...
dearer than his own life. ...
Yet after a ...
nearly two hours, victory...
in this critical state of th...
had recourse to a success...
Snatching a large bran...
dering fire in the centre'...
it to the mass of which

This resolution of the com-
mander appeared necessary from the fact that
his men were fatigued by their march through
a pathless wilderness with their provisions,
arms, &c." Accordingly on the morning of
the twenty-ninth of May, sixteen hundred thir-
ty-seven, they had proceeded directly from
Pancatuch River towards Mystic, under the
guidance of the traitor Wequash. This army
was the dark body we have seen stealing over
the hill, and, and the shadows proceeding it
were its Indian scouts.

Let us now again return to Wequash, whom
we left listening to the sounds that arrested
his attention and progress, on the tops of the
western ridge.

After having his ears greeted with a repetition of the sounds, he retraced his steps until
he met the advanced scouts of the army, and
led them to little grove beneath the ledges,
where, the whole force once arriving, they en-
camped for the night.

'Twas a bright starlight evening. The
sweet, calm river mirrored the twinkling gems
far down in its clear depths, while along its
shores the dark shadows of the trees which
lined its banks were cast far out into its stream.
At a distance below, a strong line of light was
thrown like a glittering chain across its waters,
proceeding from the Pequot Fort, and illumi-
nated the opposite hill as the setting sun had
done a short time previous. All was still save
the almost imperceptible hum made by the en-
camping army, and the sounds of revelry coming from the fort; which latter, filled the heart
of Wequash, still angry, if possible, with a
deep, burning desire for revenge. O, how he

In May of that year, the association, by means of the newspaper, did something the labor movement had not previously been able to do. The Massachusetts Corporation in Lowell had announced that its weavers would have to tend four looms instead of three and that at the same time the piece rate paid to the weaver would be reduced by one cent, a considerable sum, when weekly wages were about two dollars.

The association appointed a committee of three to draw up a pledge not to accept a fourth loom, unless the rate of pay remained the same. "Anyone violating this pledge," said the notice in the paper, "shall be published in the *Voice of Industry* as a traitor, and receive the scorn and reproach of her associates." Every weaver in the Massachusetts mill signed the pledge and kept it.

A "Female Department" featured special items of interest to women and became a means of communication between cities. The banner motto on that page read: AS IS WOMAN, SO IS THE RACE.

The farm girl had come a long way. Her factory experience had given her a feeling of independence and self-worth. In the mills and boardinghouses she developed a sense of solidarity with her working sis-

Front page of the Voice of Industry, *1846. Sarah's name appears at the top as one of the Publishing Committee.*

ters. When conditions grew worse, these women were able to join hands in protest. They realized, however, that in acting in this way, they were defying standards set for them in a man's world.

It was not seemly for a woman to draw attention to herself, but in introducing the "Female Department," Sarah promised, "It will not be neutral because it is female, but will claim to be heard on all subjects that effect her intellectual, social or religious condition." A new feminism was in the air. In two years the historic woman suffrage convention at Seneca Falls, New York, would be taking place. What is interesting is that the earliest sentiments on what the woman's role was came from working women.

They protested that marriage was considered to be the main business of a young woman, who should devote herself to nothing more than dressing, cooking and loving. If she reads, it must be light reading, not politics or history.

An article called "The Rights of Women," demands that women have the right to "buy and sell, solicit and refuse, choose and reject, as have men." As to working women, they earned far less than men, and many had families to support.

Sarah begs the operative to find time to develop her mind, no matter how tired she is. She encourages attendance at the *Voice's* improvement circle. "Do not say 'I have no time'," she entreats. If a girl gives the excuse that she can't write, why that is the reason she must try harder. Practice makes perfect. The only way to learn is to do.

In 1846, Sarah traveled a great deal, both for the association and for the *Voice*. When she was in Concord, the capital of New Hampshire, she ran into some friends from her hometown. She was almost in tears when she saw them going back to Meredith Bridge by stagecoach, leaving her behind to go about her affairs. She longed to see her "dearly beloved father and mother," whom she hadn't seen in a year.

Sarah spent some time visiting a New Hampshire state prison. She noted with interest that the prisoners, who had been sentenced to "hard work" as punishment for their crimes, worked two hours less each day than the Lowell operatives! There was no "lighting up" of oil lamps when the sky grew dark. They simply went away from their posts. "The time is not far distant," she wrote shortly afterward, "when a man would be regarded as a monster who would exact thirteen hours labor in a day from females."

Sarah had left mill work early in 1846, hoping never to return. She opened a shop on John Street with a woman friend and for a short time tried to support herself doing dressmaking and millinery work. It was to be an extremely busy year for her. In addition to her organizing work, which involved a good bit of travel, she served as delegate to several

TIME TABLE OF THE LOWELL MILLS,

Arranged to make the working time throughout the year average 11 hours per day.

TO TAKE EFFECT SEPTEMBER 21st, 1853,

The Standard time being that of the meridian of Lowell, as shown by the Regulator Clock of AMOS SANBORN, Post Office Corner, Central Street.

From March 20th to September 19th, inclusive.

COMMENCE WORK, at 6.30 A. M. LEAVE OFF WORK, at 6.30 P. M., except on Saturday Evenings.
BREAKFAST at 6 A. M.   DINNER, at 12 M.   Commence Work, after dinner, 12.45 P. M.

From September 20th to March 19th, inclusive.

COMMENCE WORK, at 7.00 A. M.   LEAVE OFF WORK, at 7.00 P. M., except on Saturday Evenings.
BREAKFAST at 6.30 A. M.   DINNER, at 12.30 P.M.   Commence Work, after dinner, 1.15 P. M.

BELLS.

From March 20th to September 19th, inclusive.

Morning Bells.	*Dinner Bells.*	*Evening Bells.*
First bell,..........4.30 A. M.	Ring out,...........12.00 M.	Ring out,...........6.30 P. M.
Second, 5.30 A. M.; Third, 6.20.	Ring in,...........12 35 P. M.	Except on Saturday Evenings.

From September 20th to March 19th, inclusive.

Morning Bells.	*Dinner Bells.*	*Evening Bells.*
First bell,..........5.00 A. M.	Ring out,...........12.30 P. M.	Ring out at..........7.00 P. M.
Second, 6.00 A. M.; Third, 6.50.	Ring in,...........1.05 P. M.	Except on Saturday Evenings.

SATURDAY EVENING BELLS.

During APRIL, MAY, JUNE, JULY, and AUGUST, Ring Out, at 6.00 P. M.
The remaining Saturday Evenings in the year, ring out as follows :

SEPTEMBER.

First Saturday, ring out 6.00 P. M.
Second " " 5.45 "
Third " " 5.30 "
Fourth " " 5.20 "

OCTOBER.

First Saturday, ring out 5.05 P. M.
Second " " 4.55 "
Third " " 4.45 "
Fourth " " 4.35 "
Fifth " " 4.25 "

NOVEMBER.

First Saturday, ring out 4.15 P. M.
Second " " 4.05 "

NOVEMBER.

Third Saturday ring out 4.00 P. M.
Fourth " " 3.55 "

DECEMBER.

First Saturday, ring out 3.50 P. M.
Second " " 3.55 "
Third " " 3.55 "
Fourth " " 4.00 "
Fifth " " 4.00 "

JANUARY.

First Saturday, ring out 4.10 P. M.
Second " " 4.15 "

JANUARY.

Third Saturday, ring out 4.25 P. M.
Fourth " " 4.35 "

FEBRUARY.

First Saturday, ring out 4.45 P. M.
Second " " 4.55 "
Third " " 5.00 "
Fourth " " 5.10 "

MARCH.

First Saturday, ring out 5.25 P. M.
Second " " 5.30 "
Third " " 5.35 "
Fourth " " 5.45 "

YARD GATES will be opened at the first stroke of the bells for entering or leaving the Mills.

*** SPEED GATES commence hoisting three minutes before commencing work.

Penhallow, Printer, Wyman's Exchange, 28 Merrimack St.

As late as 1853 mill operatives were working a twelve-hour day.

labor conventions and made a dramatic career change.

Another attempt was made to appeal to the Massachusetts legislature. The Lowell petition was a scroll 130 feet long, with forty-five hundred signatures. Petitions from other cities added ten thousand additonal names. One of the state senators who had seemed sympathetic to the labor groups, gave them no support at all when the question was brought up. The legislature ruled that it "could not deprive the citizen of his freedom of contract" and that any hampering of corporations would injure business.

Just how meaningless a citizen's "freedom of contract" was, could be illustrated in 1847, when the New Hampshire legislature passed a law making ten hours a legal day's work *in absence of a contract*. The day the law was passed all the textile mill workers in New Hampshire were fired. They were rehired only if they agreed to sign a new contract keeping the hours exactly as long as they had been! In 1848, the same thing happened in Pennsylvania.

Early in 1847, both the New England Workingmen's Association and the Female Labor Reform Association changed their names. The first became the Labor Reform League, the second the Female Labor Reform and Mutual Aid Society. The women's group was offering social benefits, such as sick leave pay, to its members and hoping to appeal to "the self-love of the operatives and to their higher natures." What seemed to be practical ideas was actually a turning away from militant action.

Is it a coincidence that this was precisely the time Sarah dropped out of labor activity? There was a rumor at the time that one of the women leaders had become ill, and some have speculated that Sarah was that leader. Others have said that she may have dropped out because she did not like the way things were going in the Massachusetts labor movement.

In 1846, Sarah had become vice-president of the Lowell Union of Associationists, the group that had been won over to the idea of living communally. The likelihood is that she had come under their influence and gave up labor activity for more glorious concerns.

The struggle for the ten-hour day became the work of politicians and liberal reformers in the fifties and sixties. It was not until 1874 that Massachusetts passed a ten-hour law, thirty years after the founding of the New England Workingmen's Association and thirty years after the ten-hour goal had been reached in the gloomy factories of old England.

Sarah's last piece in the Voice appeared in October, 1846. By then she was no longer listed as a member of the publishing committee.

Earlier, in February of 1846, after she had left the mill, Sarah had done a remarkable thing. She had become the first woman telegraph operator in the country. The Voice reported it this way:

*The Magnetic Telegraph is now completed
from this City to Boston and will be in successful operation in a few days. This enter-
prise has been prosecuted under the direction
of Mr. Paul R. George, whose democracy in
selecting a superintendent in Lowell is truly
commendable; having appointed to that
office Miss Sarah G. Bagley, one of our publishing committee. This is what we call* "the
people's" democracy, *Miss Bagley having
served ten years in the factories.*

6

What Hath God Wrought?

AMERICANS in the mid-twentieth century were fond of saying that most of the scientists who ever lived were then alive, because science had taken such a giant leap in that century. There was a similar feeling in the nineteenth century. Almost every year something new was invented. On the heels of the cotton gin, came the sewing machine and the typewriter and countless other devices that would change the daily life of every American.

One of these inventions was the "magnetic telegraph." Samuel Finley Breese Morse, the man who worked out the most successful model and raised the money and popular interest for it, started out in life as a poor and talented portrait painter. He was fascinated by electricity, a power recently discovered, that could travel over a wire of any length and get from one point to another in a fraction of a minute.

Once, on a ship voyage, he heard someone saying, "You know, a person can find out if electricity is actually being transmitted through a wire by break-ing the circuit."

"Then you might say," contributed Morse, "that the electricity is then made visible."

"Made *visible?*" The man appeared not to understand.

"What I mean is," Morse said, "that if you can control the electricity which is there at one moment, and not there at another, you can transmit intelli-gence, or information."

"Quite so, but how would you go about it?" the man asked. Morse spent most of the remainder of his life answering that question.

By the time Sarah had walked into the Lowell Telegraph Depot in February, 1846, Morse had demonstrated in the United States Supreme Court his amazing new device, sending the famous message to an assistant in Baltimore: WHAT HATH GOD WROUGHT?

The new invention was not taken too seriously. People took rifle shots at the glass knobs used as in-sulators on the telegraph wires. The original copper wires had a way of melting in the sun and had to be replaced by iron ones. There were so many failures the telegraph was labeled "arrant humbug."

But Sarah attacked her new job the way she had taken on the ten-hour movement, with energy. For several weeks she studied Morse's alphabet of dots and dashes and then set to work, taking messages on the arrival and departure of ships in Boston harbor, and other facts of interest to the local populace. Until that time "news" had been something carried by post-riders in wagons traveling from town to town. Now there was this "wonderful invention *ticking* its intelligence from point to point with a speed that makes former fables appear like prophecy," according to the local press.

Sarah operated the one-woman depot, acting as battery person, cleaning the acid cups, and as a center for the local news and part-time ticket agent for some local events. As a woman doing what was considered to be a man's job, she was the butt of some ridicule.

"The long mooted question 'Can a woman keep a secret?' will now become more interesting than ever," someone wrote in the *Boston Journal*. William Schouler's *Courier* commented cutely, "We presume the young bachelors will be sending valentines over the wires all the time." Sarah, used to far more vicious attacks, tossed these off without comment. Now, anxious to have the world see the wonders of this new invention, Sarah took part in a unique "entertainment."

August 24, 1846. Lowell's city hall is full of people who have come to witness an evening of "rational attractions" and "brilliant experiments." New scientific discoveries are presented as tricks for popular amusement.

First a five-dollar gold piece is placed in a dish. Anyone in the audience who can remove the gold piece will be able to keep it. First one person tries, then another. The coin cannot be removed because there is a magnetic machine under the dish.

Next, a balloon filled with hydrogen is sent up from the stage to the ceiling of the hall, its "car" attached by strings and filled with dolls carried with it. A dead rat is made to seem brought back to life by the power of "galvanism," or shocks administered by certain metals. A piece of iron is suspended in midair by an electrical current. But the highlight of the evening, the one for which the audience has parted with the twelve-cent admission, is Sarah Bagley's demonstration of the telegraph.

Her assistant at this exhibition is Quincy Gardner Colton. Colton, who had started in life as an impoverished weaver, had gone to New York City to study medicine. While there he heard Morse lecture to a packed audience at the Broadway Tabernacle, reading to the cheering crowd the first telegraph message to reach New York: CANST THOU SEND LIGHTNINGS, THAT THEY MAY GO, AND SAY UNTO THEE, HERE WE ARE? Colton introduced himself to Morse and eventually asked to be instructed in the workings of the magnetic telegraph.

He became so skilled that Morse gave him a letter "of unqualified recommendation" so that he could lecture around the country. That same year Colton had also discovered the strange effect of nitrous oxide, or "laughing gas," when inhaled. Together with a dentist, Colton was able to start a tooth extraction business that became extremely profitable, at two dollars for the first extraction and one dollar for each additional tooth. At Lowell he was merely Sarah Bagley's aide. Sarah sat in the front of the hall with her telegraph and Colton placed himself in the back of the hall with his.

People from the audience were invited to whisper "messages" to Colton, which he tapped out with his signal key. A few seconds later Sarah drew the tape with its dots and dashes from her register and repeated the message. Then Sarah stood up and explained to the thousand people in the audience how the mechanism worked. The audience stood up and applauded for a long time.

Sarah didn't realize that in taking her post as superintendent of the depot, she was opening up a new area of work for women. By 1853, over fifty women were employed by one telegraph line alone.

Sarah stayed with this work for two years. The Hamilton Corporation records of 1848 show her returning to the weave room of Mill B for five months. The circumstances of this change are not known. It may have been that mill work paid more and she was in need of the extra wages.

In September of that year she was called home to the bedside of her father, who was dying of typhus.

She left Lowell, never to return. When her brother died in 1854, his estate reported "no relations" except his aged mother. This was proven to be inaccurate, but there are no further records of Sarah Bagley's life.

There were other militant and outspoken women to take her place in the Female Labor Reform Association when she dropped out of activity. There was the Eliza Hemingway who had testified at the 1845 hearings, who was also involved in the cooperative store movement. A Mary Eastman took Sarah's place as president of the association. Huldah Stone, who had served as secretary and had written eloquent pieces for the *Voice of Industry*, was to migrate to the new textile town of Lawrence, Massachusetts, where she applied for a job as a boardinghouse keeper. Unknown to her, a letter had preceded her to Lawrence from the agent of the Middlesex mill. It urged agents not to hire Huldah—"a radical of the worst sort & late editress of the *Voice of Industry*."

The *Voice of Industry* itself became the *New Era of Industry*, and survived a few years as the voice of the utopian reformers who had so beguiled the workers and their leader Sarah Bagley.

No voice is wholly lost. As the fuller history of labor and of women in the United States is revealed in new researches, Bagley will be seen as one of the true heroines of her time.

Bibliography

SARAH G. BAGLEY
SOURCES

Stern, Madeleine B. *We the Women: Career Firsts of*
    Nineteenth-Century America. New York, 1963.
Zwarg, Christina Lynne. "Woman as Wife or Worker:
    the Success and Failure of Feminism in the Lowell
    Female Labor Reform Association, 1841–1845."
    Master's thesis, Brown University, Providence,
    Rhode Island, 1975.
Voice of Industry (Fitchburg, Lowell, Boston) 1845–1848.
Wright, Helena. "Sarah G. Bagley, a Biographical Note."
    Labor History, Vol. 20, 1979.

BOOKS BY LUCY LARCOM

As It Is in Heaven. Boston, 1891.
At the Beautiful Gate, and Other Songs of Faith.
    Boston, 1892.
Childhood Songs. Boston, 1875.
Easter Gleams. Boston, 1890.
An Idyl of Work. Boston, 1875.
Leila Among the Mountains. Boston, 1861.
Lottie's Thought-book. Philadelphia, 1858.
A New England Girlhood, Outlined From Memory.
    Boston, 1889. (Reprinted: New York, 1961)
Poems. Boston, 1869.
Poetical Works (Household Edition). Boston, 1885.
Ships in the Mist, and Other Stories. Boston, 1860.
Similitudes. Boston, 1854.
The Unseen Friend. Boston, 1892.
Wild Roses of Cape Ann, and Other Poems. Boston, 1881

SOURCES

Lucy Larcom papers can be found mainly at the following:
    Beverly Historical Society, Beverly, Massachusetts
    Essex Institute, Salem, Massachusetts
    Massachusetts Historical Society, Boston,
        Massachusetts
    University of Virginia Library, Barrett Collection,
        Manuscript Dept., Charlottesville, Virginia
    Wheaton College Library, Norton, Massachusetts

Addison, Daniel Dulaney. *Lucy Larcom: Life, Letters, and Diary*. Boston, 1895.

American Literary Manuscripts: a Checklist of Holdings in Academic, Historical and Public Libraries in the United States. Austin, Texas, 1960.

Bennett, Whitman. *Whittier, Bard of Freedom*. Chapel Hill, North Carolina, 1941.

Blanck, Jacob. *Bibliography of American Literature*. New Haven, Connecticut, 1955–1973. Vol. 5.

Pickard, Samuel T. *Life and Letters of John Greenleaf Whittier*. Boston, 1895.

Spaulding, Charles Warren. *The Spalding Memorial: a Geneological History of Edward Spalding*. Chicago, 1897.

Woodberry, George Edward. *Literary Memoirs of the Nineteenth Century*. New York, 1921.

Ernest, Joseph M. "Whittier and the 'Feminine Fifties.' " *American Literature*, Vol. 28, May, 1956.

Larcom, Lucy. "Among Lowell Mill Girls, a Reminiscence." *Atlantic Monthly*, Vol. 48, November, 1881.

Larcom, Lucy. "Lucy Larcom letters: extracts from the Collection in the Library of the Essex Institute." *Essex Institute Historical Collections*, Vol. 68, 1932.

The Rushlight. "Special Number in Memory of Lucy Larcom" (edited by Susan Hayes Ward). Boston, 1894.

Shepard, Grace. "Letters of Lucy Larcom to the Whittiers." *New England Quarterly*, Vol. 3, July, 1930.

Our Young Folks: an Illustrated Magazine for Boys and
  Girls (Boston) 1865–1873; also Yesterday's Children:
  an Anthology Compiled from the Pages of Our
  Young Folks (edited by John Morton Blum). Boston,
  1959.

BOOKS BY
HARRIET HANSON ROBINSON

Captain Mary Miller. Boston, 1887.
Early Factory Labor in New England. Boston, 1883.
Loom and Spindle; or, Life Among the Lowell Mill Girls,
  with a Sketch of The Lowell Offering and some of
  its Contributors. Boston, 1898 (Reprinted: Kailua,
  Hawaii, 1976).
Massachusetts in the Woman Suffrage Movement: a
  General Political Legal and Legislative History
  from 1774–1881. Boston, 1881.
"Memoir of 'Warrington,'" in "Warrington"
  Pen-Portraits, by William Stevens Robinson. Boston,
  1877.
The New Pandora, a Drama. New York, 1889

SOURCES

Harriet Hanson Robinson papers can be found at the
  Arthur and Elizabeth Schlesinger Library on the
  History of Women in America, Radcliffe College,

Cambridge, Massachusetts (Robinson-Shattuck Papers, Collection A-80).

Bushman, Claudia L. *"A Good Poor Man's Wife," Being a Chronicle of Harriet Hanson Robinson and her Family in Nineteenth-Century New England.* Hanover, New Hampshire, 1981.

Merk, Lois B. "Massachusetts and the Woman-Suffrage Movement." Ph.D. dissertation, Radcliffe College, 1958.

Rothman, Ellen Kate. "Harriet Hanson Robinson: a Search for Satisfaction in the 19th-Century Woman's Movement." Undergraduate thesis, Radcliffe College, 1973.

GENERAL

America's Working Women (edited by Rosalyn Baxandall, Linda Gordon and Susan Reverby). New York, 1976.

Beecher, Catherine Esther. *The Evils Suffered by American Women and Children, the Causes and the Remedy.* New York,1846.

Chevalier, Michel. *Society, Manners and Politics in the United States: Letters on North America.* Boston, 1839.

Dickens, Charles. *American Notes for General Circulation.* Boston, 1881.

A Documentary History of American Industrial Society
(edited by John R. Commons and Associates). Vol.
7, 8. Cleveland, Ohio, 1910.

Dublin, Thomas. *Women at Work: the Transformation
of Work and Community in Lowell, Massachusetts,
1826–1860.* New York, 1979.

Flexner, Eleanor. *A Century of Struggle: the Woman's
Rights Movement in the United States.* New York,
1973.

Foner, Philip S. *The Factory Girls: a Collection of
Writings on Life and Struggles in New England
Factories of the 1840s by the Factory Girls
Themselves.* Urbana, Illinois, 1977.

Hymowitz, Carol and Michaele Weissman. *A History of
Women in America.* New York, 1978.

Josephson, Hannah. *The Golden Threads: New
England's Mill Girls and Magnates.* New York, 1949.

Kessler-Harris, Alice. *Out to Work: a History of Wage-
earning Women in the United States.* New York,
1982.

McCauley, Elfrieda B. "The New England Mill Girls:
Feminine Influence in the Development of Public
Libraries in New England." D.L.S. dissertation,
Columbia University, 1971.

Miles, Henry A. *Lowell, as it Was, and as it Is.* Lowell,
1846.

*Notable American Women: a Biographical Dictionary,
1607–1950.* (edited by Edward T. James).
Cambridge, Massachusetts, 1971. Vol. 1–3.

Ware, Norman. *The Industrial Worker, 1840–1860.*
Boston, 1924.

Wertheimer, Barbara Meyer. *We Were There: the
Story of Working Women in America.* New York,
1977.

Lowell Offering (Lowell) October, 1840–December,
1845, *also The Lowell Offering: Writings by New
England Mill Women, 1840–1845* (edited by Benita
Eisler). New York, 1977.

New England Offering (Lowell) April, 1848–February,
1850.

Operatives' Magazine (Lowell) April, 1841–March, 1842.

FOR CHILDREN

Cahn, William and Rhoda. *No Time for School, No
Time for Play: the Story of Child Labor in America.*
New York, 1972.

Holland, Ruth. *Mill Child.* New York, 1970.

Index